VOICES OF AMERICA

Jewish
Maxwell Street
Stories

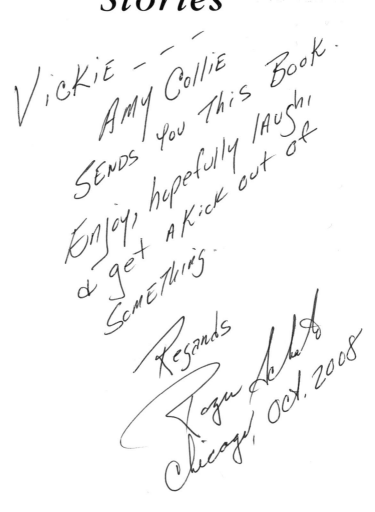

VickiE – – –
Amy Collie
Sends you This Book.
Enjoy, hopefully lAugh,
& get A Kick out of
SomEThing.

Regards

Roger Schatz
Chicago, Oct. 2008

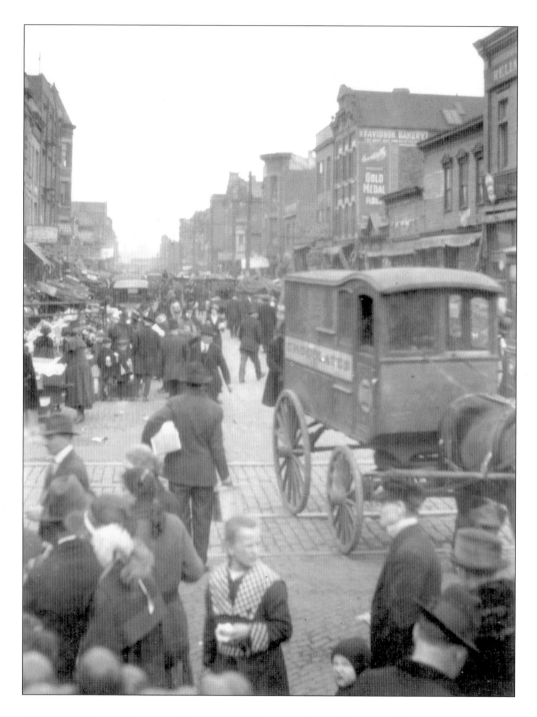

Maxwell Street Looking East from Halsted, 1919. *(Courtesy of University of Illinois at Chicago Library, Department of Special Collections.)*

Cover: Background photo from the David R. Phillips Collection. Inset photo courtesy of the Chicago Historical Society.

VOICES OF AMERICA

Jewish Maxwell Street Stories

Shuli Eshel and Roger Schatz

ARCADIA

Published by Arcadia Publishing,
Charleston SC, Chicago IL, Portsmouth NH, San Francisco CA

Printed in the United States of America

Library of Congress Catalog Card Number: 2004100276

For all general information contact Arcadia Publishing at:
Telephone 843-853-2070
Fax 843-853-0044
E-mail sales@arcadiapublishing.com
For customer service and orders:
Toll-Free 1-888-313-2665

Visit us on the Internet at http://www.arcadiapublishing.com

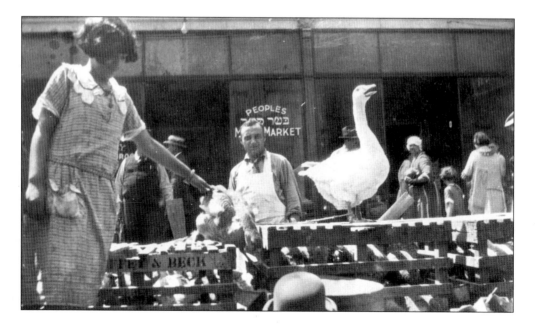

DUCK, 1920s. *Poultry shoppers on old Maxwell Street would choose the bird they wanted. Kosher butchers would then slaughter and prepare it. (Courtesy of University of Illinois at Chicago Library, Department of Special Collections.)*

Contents

Contents, Continued

Acknowledgments

The wrecking ball has swung on historic Maxwell Street. To see the area today, with acres of new condominiums and only a few preserved old buildings, it would be impossible to know that for most of a century, it was home to a vibrant, eclectic, stunning humanity, all surrounded by one of the greatest bazaars in the world.

Jewish Maxwell Street Stories follows the success of my documentary, *Maxwell Street: A Living Memory, The Jewish Experience in Chicago*. If it were not for Elliot Zashin's initiative as the treasurer of the Maxwell Street Historic Preservation Coalition (MSHPC), the documentary and the book would not exist. I would like to extend my sincerest thanks to Elliot, who worked tirelessly as executive producer for the film, and gave valuable comments and help for the book. Also special thanks to the other officers and directors of the MSHPC: Charles Cowdery, Steven Balkin, and Lori Grove for their enthusiasm and support. Lori Grove and Laura Kamedulski's book, *Chicago's Maxwell Street*, is one of the titles in Arcadia Publishing's Images of America photographic series, and has been a useful source for this book. Thank you also to Dr. Irving Cutler for granting us the extensive interview that provided so many facts, names, and locales that became central to the film and book. I am grateful to Russell Lewis, Director for Collections and Research, and Rob Medina of the Chicago Historical Society. They have granted permission to use rare photographs. Also, thanks to Patricia Bakunas of the library at the University of Illinois at Chicago, for the use of their images.

Thank you to photographer Jack Davis for some general pictures. Thanks also to Fay Katlin for providing a photo from the David R. Phillips Collection, used as the background image for the book cover and excerpts from the personal Maxwell Street memoir she sent for the story, "Mandolins to Medicine Balls." Thanks also go to Shirley Leavitt for bringing attention to her late husband, Sol's journal, which is quoted extensively in the story, "Leavitt's Restaurant and Delicatessen." In the story, "Sharpshooter," Harriet Karm Berman supplied a photo and excerpts from an article entitled, "The Street," which she initially published in the Chicago Jewish Historical Society's Spring, 2002 edition of *Chicago Jewish History*. I am grateful to Mr. William W. Garfield who took time to write a short piece that so thoroughly captures what Maxwell Street was all about.

To Sheldon Good, Ferne Stone, Gene Mackevich, Seymour Persky, Jerry and Burt Weinstein, Jordon Ross, Seymour DeKoven, Irving Federman, Larry Lerner, Herb Kanter, and the Bublick and Mages families, my deep gratitude for the cooperation and encouragement that went along with their stories. And, certainly, warm thanks to all the individuals from the last Maxwell Street generations, their children, and other relatives, who shared their memories and photos. Not all could be acknowledged here, nor included in the book. However, I will always be thrilled by their responses to the documentary and the excitement they exhibited in providing their Maxwell Street stories.

Roger Schatz and I are indebted to John Pearson, publisher, and Samantha Gleisten, editor, of Arcadia Publishing for recognizing that we had a treasure in hand that belonged in Arcadia's *Voices of America* series. We appreciate the guidance they and their staff provided.

Any omissions in these acknowledgements are unintentional. All who called, wrote, contributed, and put up with my many requests, please know that you are in my heart.

–Shuli Eshel
Chicago,Ill.
December, 2003

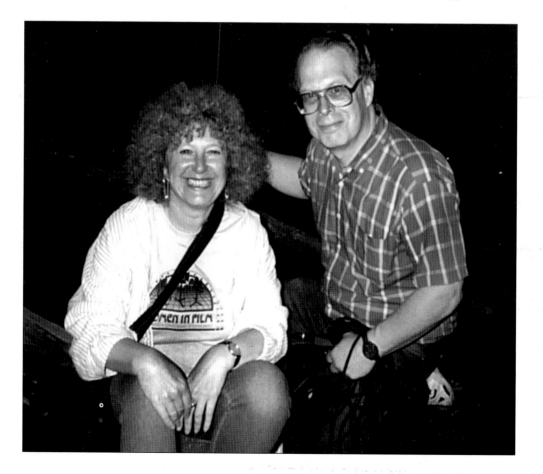

SHULI ESHEL AND ROGER SCHATZ. *Authors Shuli Eshel and Roger Schatz on a break from field production of Ms. Eshel's documentary,* Maxwell Street: A Living Memory. The Jewish Experience in Chicago.

Introduction
PART 1

Maxwell Street was one of the first places I learned of when I came to Chicago from Israel in 1989. In fact, I included scenes of Maxwell Street in the first documentary I was making in the city for the Chicago Women's Caucus for Art entitled, *Perception of the "Other": Exploring Cultural Diversity.*

So, it did not come as a great surprise when my friend Elliot Zashin, the treasurer of the Maxwell Street Historic Preservation Coalition, called me in the summer of 1999 with a request:

"We have not been successful in saving Maxwell Street. Would you be interested in helping us preserve some of the memories of the Jewish immigrants who created the Maxwell Street market? Would you produce a documentary?"

My answer was an immediate "Yes." I knew instinctively that the Jews of Chicago, whom I considered my people, had an important story to tell.

It took two-and-a-half years to produce the half-hour documentary, *Maxwell Street: A Living Memory, The Jewish Experience in Chicago.* It took that long because really, it was a three person operation: Elliot Zashin, Roger Schatz, my business partner at Cavalcade Communications Group, Inc., and myself. Initially, we received a grant from the Illinois Arts Council for fifteen hundred dollars. Eventually, with the help of a grant from the Illinois Humanities Council and donors from the Jewish community, we were able to complete the work.

As producer and director, I first looked at the story as one of "rags to riches," because I knew that many of the most influential people in Chicago's Jewish community came from Maxwell Street. But as we collected the many stories, I realized they painted a much more complex picture. The Eastern European Jewish immigrants that came to Chicago after the Great Fire of 1871 were fleeing from the pogroms and poverty. They didn't speak English, and they were used to a very Jewish way of life. The cultural adjustment was huge as they struggled to raise their children with Jewish values and give them a good education. In the end, the documentary integrated stories told by those children, to develop a context explaining what a Maxwell Street background meant in the pursuit of the American dream.

Now that historic Maxwell Street has been completely demolished, this book is even more important. I had collectd thirty-two hours of interviews. I felt that there was a need to expand on the stories presented in the film, and preserve others that emerged in the significant wake the documentary created. I am very grateful that Roger Schatz collaborated with me in preserving the historical, often amazing Jewish Maxwell Street Stories.

–Shuli Eshel
Chicago,Ill.
December, 2003

Introduction
PART 2

For most who remember the shopping on Maxwell Street in its halcyon days, the images and memories are of the bargains, the food, the Blues, and the knowledge that something extraordinary could occur at any moment.

For those who did the selling, it was much more.

By becoming the center of commerce for most of the Jewish immigrants who arrived in Chicago from the late-19th century until after the Holocaust, Maxwell Street proved a single inventory store where shelves were stocked with the American dream. The contents of that dream were always freedom and opportunity. On Maxwell Street, those ingredients were mixed into what many on the street might have called a "mish-mosch" of religion, tradition, assimilation, entrepreneurship, and extremely hard work. Included in the recipe were tears, joy, disappointment, love, devotion, ideas, nerve, tolerance, success, failure, trust, and honor. However the ingredients were added, whatever the order, the desired outcome of the dream was survival, growth, stability, and a foundation from which the children and grandchildren of the early Maxwell Street generations could flourish.

As Shuli noted, those children and grandchildren dominate this book. A select group of men and women whose families came from Maxwell Street were included in Shuli's documentary, *Maxwell Street: A Living Memory, The Jewish Experience In Chicago.* Since the 2002 premier of the documentary, literally hundreds have come forward to tell their Maxwell Street stories. The response to the documentary is still reverberating. People have not stopped communicating their experiences on Maxwell Street with us.

There are thousands of Maxwell Street stories, and no doubt tens of thousands yet untold. Over the decades millions of people went to Maxwell Street. It was a place where mere moments became lifelong memories. Would that all those stories could be documented.

Unlike the documentary, the book is more of an anthology which puts emphasis on the individuality of the stories. Still, as in the film, it is impossible not to be moved by the depth of influence Maxwell Street had on shaping lives. Some stories are included because they are simply funny or inspiring or sad, or just because we were so impressed. We hope our tastes on that account are agreeable with your own.

While the focus of the stories in the book, given the obvious title, is on the Jewish generations, as it was in the documentary, there are compelling stories of non-Jews, as well. Nate Duncan's story is tied directly to Ben Lyon's story. Also, the story of Sammy Skobel shows perfectly, that you didn't have to be Jewish to grasp the promise that Maxwell Street's opportunities and influence offered. Retired Chicago police officer Patrick Angelo provides insight into the market's dynamics, which he experienced for almost 40 years on the beat.

You can write a book about the stories of African Americans on Maxwell Street. You can write one about the gypsies on Maxwell Street, or the Koreans or Hispanics who came to operate businesses there. But, the Jewish experience molded the area, it seeped into Chicago's and the nation's fabric. Even now, after the last wrecking ball slammed into the last old brick wall, Maxwell Street is known to many, affectionately or not, as "Jew Town."

For readers unfamiliar with the area, there is a single street called Maxwell Street. But it grew to become a location rather than just a street. References to Maxwell Street evolved to define a huge market area that might accurately be measured as at least a square mile in size, encompassing many streets and thoroughfares. The Maxwell Street area was only a few blocks from Chicago's Loop, but by contrast, it was another world.

As a youth, my father, Peter Schatz, lived close to Maxwell Street at 14th and Throop. He graduated from near-by Medill High School. In its last two decades, I had shopped on Maxwell Street, and spent time there working on stories I covered as a reporter. I thought of my dad whenever I went there.

But, my connection with Maxwell Street began to expand significantly as Shuli's documentary took form. It was late and its fate was sealed, but the place started getting into my soul. As I photographed the demolition of the area, when I saw a floor mosaic of the Star of David crushed by the jaws of a front loader ripping one of the last buildings along Halsted Street, I again thought of my father, and was finally struck with the realization that I was working on a labor of love.

This book not only allows for telling more Maxwell Street stories in ways a film cannot, it allowed me to continue my affair with the subject matter. Publication of this book doesn't end the affair. I have found a way to carry it on. Whenever I drive down Halsted Street and approach Maxwell Street, I don't see brand new condominiums and light pole banners proclaiming University Village as Chicago's newest and best place to live. I see ghosts. I feel ghosts. I can inhale the aroma of red hots and grilled onions. I worry some guy will pull me into a store and talk me into buying something I don't need. I hear the salesman who sold me a sport coat from the "gold room" in the back say in Yiddish, 'Trog Es Gezunterheyd . . . Wear it in good health.'

The editing of the stories has been carefully done. Story sources have been checked and double checked to ensure no misunderstandings. Quotes of the storytellers have, at times, been edited to allow written word clarity that often was missing or confusing in the verbatim descriptions given in the interviews.

–Roger Schatz
Chicago, Ill.
December, 2003

MAXWELL STREET, 1920. *Where else could you find a pair of used long-johns displayed on a telephone pole? Where else would someone be looking to buy them? (Courtesy of University of Illinois at Chicago Library, Department of Special Collections.)*

I.

First You Survive

BERTHA'S BOY

When Bertha Persky had cleaned and mended clothing she bought second-hand, she took a 22-pound iron off her wood-burning stove to press the items before heading to Maxwell Street to sell them third-hand.

Mrs. Persky's son, Seymour, was born in Chicago in 1922, and his earliest recollections of his mother's labors and the life she led with him, his brother Sam, and sister Kati, go back to when he was about five years old.

"We lived in a store. My mother had a rummage shop at 1432 West 14th Street, and we lived in back of the store. We didn't even have a floor. The floor was a dirt floor. And the rent was fourteen dollars a month. And, she called it Bertha's Rummage Store. On Sundays we would go to Maxwell Street where it was absolutely vibrant and thriving. There was anything and everything for sale. And second-hand clothing found a ready market in those days. And, of course, my mother was very gifted with mending and patching, so consequently, for a dollar-and-a-half, you could get a pair of pants."

Seymour Persky's humble beginnings are not at all atypical for so many Jewish young men who later became highly successful lawyers, doctors, or business leaders. Pulling a little red wagon filled with the used clothing his mother sold, made him, he said, a better lawyer.

BERTHA PERSKY'S IRON. Mrs. Persky lifted this 22-pound iron thousands of times to press the used clothing which she sold on Maxwell Street to support her family. (Courtesy of Eshel Productions.)

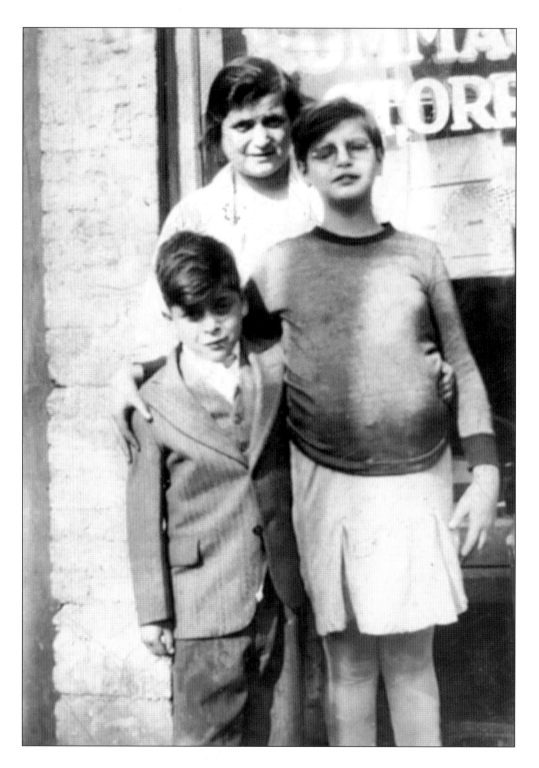

BERTHA PERSKY WITH SON, SEYMOUR AND DAUGHTER, KATI IN FRONT OF HER RUMMAGE STORE IN 1932. *Mrs. Persky made a meager living repairing and cleaning used clothing to sell on Maxwell Street. The children helped her sell the merchandise. (Courtesy of Seymour Persky.)*

SEYMOUR PERSKY, AGE SEVEN, IN 1929. *Persky remembers he was blowing on his finger after watching Charlie Chaplin do the same thing in a film. (Courtesy of Seymour Persky.)*

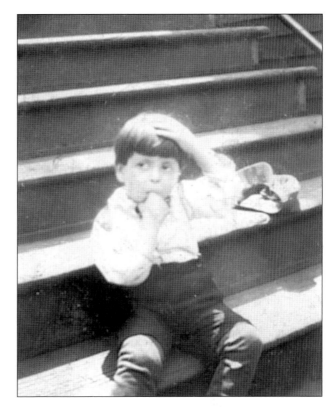

"It impacted my whole life because in my practice of law, I dare say that so much of it was negotiation. And I've been negotiating all my life. I negotiated with my big brother, Sam, so that he wouldn't hit me too many times for minor infractions. I negotiated with my mother about things. And some of the negotiations are from what I saw on Maxwell Street, and the sport of negotiations, as the thrill of besting your opponent. This had a big influence, and it gave me an absolute involvement with being Jewish. I say that it's the fabric of my personality, and my being a Jew in a Christian world."

Persky's father was almost never around when he was young. His father spent many years in England, having left Chicago to transact business that failed and left him stranded overseas. It was Persky's mother who led him to Maxwell Street.

"I would pull the little red wagon with the second-hand pants. And in the wintertime, we used a sled. My mother would enter into a conference with the market master and give him a couple of dollars. If you wanted a good location, you paid in accordance to the location of where your stand was at. And so, consequently, she would sell the trousers, and in that way, we eked out an existence.

"I can tell you that they were very, very hard times. As the great Jewish writer, Sholom Aleichem said, 'With God's help, we starved regularly.' "

Persky used the G-I Bill to get his education. He went to junior college then Roosevelt and DePaul Universities. He not only has been before the bar, he became one of Chicago's most prominent architectural historians. He is a fellow of the Society of Architectural Historians, serves on the Board of Overseers at the Illinois Institute of Technology, sits on the Landmarks Commission of the City of Chicago, and is on the Advisory Board of the Chicago Architectural Foundation.

SEYMOUR PERSKY, 1999. *"On Maxwell Street, the best merchandise was knowledge." (Courtesy of Eshel Productions.)*

Persky's Maxwell Street experience provided the dynamics that later directed his many capabilities.

"I had a rich cultural experience in Maxwell Street, and it gave me a hunger for culture and knowledge. I remember very well the great statement, 'Toyre iz di beste s'choyre,' the best merchandise in the world is knowledge." *

The poverty Persky's family experienced in his youth, despite his mother's constant efforts, influenced his significant involvement in Jewish charitible activities.

"We were the recipients of charity when they would come to our house and bring matzos for Passover. Well, I figured that they gave us a little bit, maybe we should give it back. And my own ideas are that you only really keep what you give away."

Persky's father returned home in time for the 1933 Chicago World's Fair and worked as a tailor in a Jackson Boulevard pants factory called Rosen Brothers until his death in 1957. Ultimately, Bertha Persky and her children escaped the second-hand/third-hand life on Maxwell Street and settled further west in the Douglas Park area at Douglas Boulevard and Homan Avenue. They owned the building they lived in. Seymour helped them buy it.

"Survival. It toughens you," Seymour Persky said assuredly. "You are pretty tough if you can survive Maxwell Street."

Toyre iz di beste s'choyre translates literally from the Yiddish as, *"Torah is the best merchandise."*

"If you wanted to eat regularly, you had to make a living. You learned all the tricks of the trade, of being a hustler on Maxwell Street. I quit school when I was 14 to help out my parents, 'cuz there was five of us children. And I think my education far exceeds any college education that I could have gotten. You become street smart."

–Leonard Genender

Leonard Genender lived a true Maxwell Street life. With his brothers he would keep a close eye on the various items his father sold off a pushcart. Occasionally, he had to run down a thief who stole a pair of gloves or a watch. Genender later operated his own pushcart, selling everything from razor blades to one-jewel watches. Then, in 1939 he opened his own store at 1356 South Halsted, just a few steps from the intersection with Maxwell Street.

"I sold all kinds of notions and novelties and one-jewel watches which I bought from Switzerland for two-dollars and sixty five cents apiece. I would sell street peddlers the watches for three-and-a-half dollars apiece. The peddlers used to go out on Maxwell Street and hustle the watches. They would have them on their wrist all the way up to their arm.

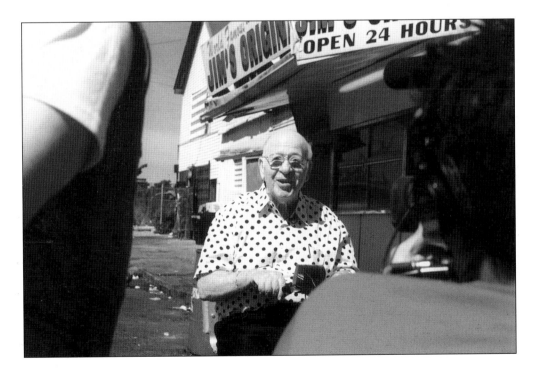

LEONARD GENENDER, 1999. *Maxwell Street was Genender's lifeline. For almost 50 years, he sold everything from notions to one-jewel watches. Street vendors recognized him and greeted him warmly on his visit to the area for interviews during production of the documentary, "Maxwell Street: A Living Memory. The Jewish Experience in Chicago." (Photo by Roger Schatz.)*

And when they would sell off their supply, I would send my son out with more watches to replenish their stock and sell them more watches. They would hang $150 or $200 price tags on them. And, of course, there were countless ways that they made money aside from the high price tags, telling their customers this is a $100 watch or a $200 watch, and they would even take five-dollars for a sale if they had to, because they still realized a dollar-and-a-half profit."

Genender realized very acceptable profits from that kind of business. He remembers a Sunday when he grossed $12,000, his best single day ever.

"I used to put out watches with the name Cimega . . . C-I-M-E-G-A. And what the peddlers would do, they would take the crystal off, take a black pen and make an "O" out of the "C" and suddenly they had an Omega watch.

"I was an entrepreneur when I was nine years old selling shopping bags on Maxwell Street. So, learning business and what to sell and all the little tricks of the business came naturally."

One of those tricks backfired on Genender when a man from the government walked into his store.

"I used to buy the little red jewels that go into a watch. I bought the jewels for three cents apiece. I would take 16 of the jewels and put them on a piece of scotch tape, open up the back of a one-jewel watch, stick the 16 jewels inside, and it was a one-jewel plus 16, that made it 17 jewels. And I used to have it printed 17 jewels on the face of the watch. So, one day, a well-dressed gentleman came along into my store and flashed a gold badge, and said he was from the Federal Trade Commission. He said, 'You're selling one-jewel watches and you're calling them 17 jewels.' I said, 'Of course they have 17 jewels in them. There's 17 in the back.' He said, 'But they're non-working jewels.' He gave me a cease and desist order, so, of course, that was the end of that escapade."

"**B**lood Money."

That's how sisters Marilyn Kalinsky Goldman and Jackie Abrams described what their parents and grandparents earned from arduous labors selling underwear on Maxwell Street.

"It was a very hard way to make a living," Marilyn Goldman said. "They made money down there. It was blood money."

"They really worked hard," Marilyn continued. "They were up at four in the morning, no matter what the weather was, they would be down there. If it was hot, they were down there. If it was cold, they were down there. When they had riots when Martin Luther King was shot, they were down there."

Jackie Abrams was down there too, working with her father and mother.

"I remember one year we were going to a funeral, it must have been 80 below zero,

RUBIN FINK AND WILLIAM KALINSKY. Both Rubin Fink, left, and William Kalinsky dropped dead of heart attacks on Maxwell Street. Respectively, they were the grandfather and father of Marilyn Kalinsky Goldman and Jackie Abrams. (Courtesy of Marilyn Kalinsky Goldman.)

and my mother diverted to Maxwell Street to sell leg warmers, and we sold them out in thirty minutes."

"Watching my parents work so hard," Jackie said, "it was truly blood money . . . I told my children money doesn't grow on trees. You want it, you've got to work for it."

Surely, not all who labored on Maxwell Street would describe their incomes as blood money. But Ms. Goldman and Ms. Abrams have good cause. In 1955, their grandfather, Rubin Fink died of a heart attack while laboring on Maxwell Street. In 1981, their father, William Kalinsky died of a heart attack, on the job at Maxwell and Halsted.

MAXWELL STREET LOOKING WEST FROM UNION AVENUE IN THE 1960S. The lure of the bargain and extraordinary food kept crowds coming even as businesses began to close. (Courtesy of photographer Jack Davis.)

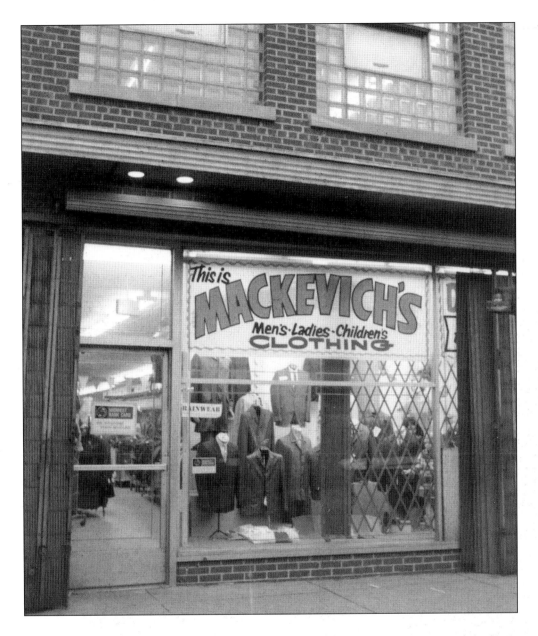

MACKEVICH'S DEPARTMENT STORE. *Mackevich's Department Store grew into one of the largest businesses in the Maxwell Street Market. Gene Mackevich estimates the family name was on the street for 75 years. (Courtesy of Gene Mackevich.)*

COCK-EYED CHUTZPAH

The big three-day promotion was over at Mackevich's Department Store on Maxwell Street. The band from Boys Town in Mexico had been a big hit. Thousands of shoppers came for the bargains, the free food, the dancing, everything. Gene Mackevich had joined the business after finishing college. Like all the Mackevich employees, the big event had left him drained.

"Everybody was wiped out," Gene laughed. "We are very tired. We are turning out the lights, we are closing the doors, we are going home. We are totally out of it. Telephone rings. A lady, Spanish-speaking lady, bought one of our dining room sets. If you bought a dining room set we gave away free, a parrot and a birdcage. When she got home she saw that the bird was cross-eyed. So, she called to complain that we should come down at seven o'clock on a Saturday night and bring her a parrot that was not cross-eyed. The person who answered the phone, Sy Newman said, 'Oh, I am so glad you called. You have made my day. We have been looking for the cross-eyed bird because it is historically famous, and it is worth so much . . . !' Click. She never called back."

You learned to think fast on Maxwell Street. You needed chutzpah.

Chutzpah has taken its place in the American vernacular, one of many Yiddish words or terms that have crossed-over. Among its definitions are nerve, gall, and brazenness. In her 1970 book, *The Taste of Yiddish,* Lillian Mermin Feinsilver surmises that the Jews' familiarity with God might explain chutzpah. "If you can argue with God, what else can't you do?"

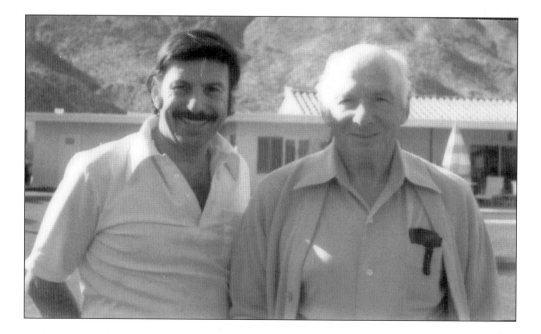

GENE AND IRA MACKEVICH. *Gene Mackevich joined his father, Ira in the family business after college in 1953. What became a Maxwell Street anchor store began in 1908 when Ira's father, Isadore Mackevich, bought and sold railroad salvage. (Courtesy of Gene Mackevich.)*

Gene Mackevich learned chutzpah was imperative for success on Maxwell Street. Qualities like that, said Mackevich, led his grandfather, Isadore, in 1908, to take a small railroad salvage business and work it and grow it into one of the true department stores on Maxwell Street.

"He started from scratch; no capital. Just guts, determination, and his own wit. He would buy out salvage merchandise. The way he would do it is he'd walk into a warehouse, or there would be a train wreck, and he didn't even know what he was bidding on. He would just set a price and make sure that everything in that pile was going to be part of the transaction. He did everything by his guts. Sometimes he won, sometimes he lost. Sometimes what he paid for was over-priced, and sometimes under-priced. But, the point is, everyday was a new risk. Everyday was a new challenge. No two days, obviously, were the same."

Ira Mackevich, Gene's father, entered the business in 1929. Gene spent many days on Maxwell Street as a youth, but the family lived on the city's north side and he seldom worked the store. He joined the business after graduating from the University of Michigan in 1953.

"Three generations," Mackevich said. I would say that we had probably 75 years actively involved on the street."

Having one of the biggest businesses in the market area didn't mean the Mackevich family was wealthy.

"The irony is, in the early days, this is a very gradual, gradual process and everything was relative. My grandfather worked, let us say, until his death in 1948, for let's say close to 50 years, and when he died, yes, there was food on the table, and nobody went hungry, but he was not a rich man. And, basically, he was just a hard-working, I would say middle-class businessman who lived by his wit."

Mackevich credits his father, Ira, with shaping the business into what became one of the centers of Maxwell Street commerce.

"Dad was a big transition for the business. I would say in the years that he was active after my grandfather died, he maintained the ongoing flow of the business. The business really started to blossom in the late fifties through the sixties. I would say in the early fifties we had about a dozen employees in the whole operation. At the height of the operation, in the good season, the holiday season, was as many as 175 to 200 employees.

"Over a period of years my grandfather and father expanded our location, all in one place, but we kept on buying new land and new buildings adjacent to where we had our business. Many people that were familiar with our store called us, in those days, the Marshall Field's of Maxwell Street."

Mackevich's was a department store in every sense of the word.

"Some of the departments we had in our department store, we started with a regular grocery store, and it became one of the first supermarkets in the city of Chicago.

We had one of the first self-service meat departments in the city, self-service produce. We had an appliance department, both small appliances and large appliances. We had a total furniture store as big as most of the furniture stores today. We had a package liquor store, we had a jewelry department, we had a toy department around the holiday seasons, we had a men's, ladies' and children's clothing department. In a sense, there was nothing we didn't have. In addition to that, through the years, in the mid-fifties, we started a dealer acceptance program, or I should say a dealer acceptance corporation, where we bought paper from other dealers that would finance customer's purchases in such things as furniture and major appliances. We also had a small loan department right there on the premises.

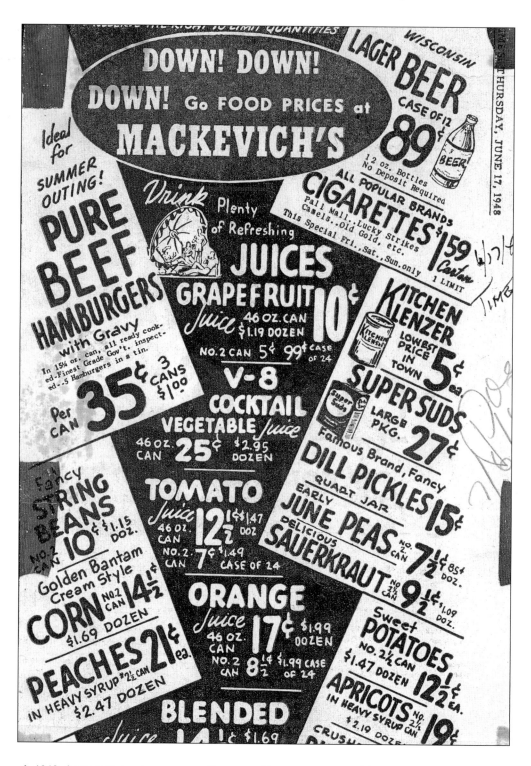

A 1948 ADVERTISEMENT FOR THE GROCERY DEPARTMENT AT MACKEVICH'S DEPARTMENT STORE. This is one of the last ads Isadore Mackevich placed before his death. His son, Ira, expanded the store significantly in later years. (Courtesy of Gene Mackevich.)

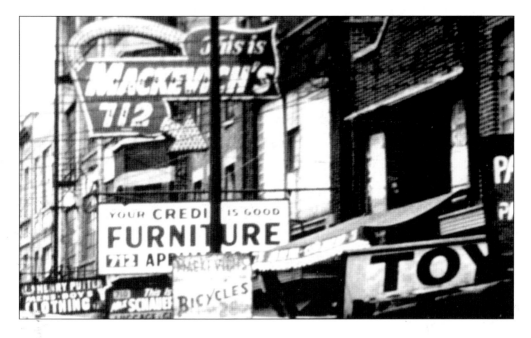

MACKEVICH SIGN. *Mackevich's had one of the few electric signs on Maxwell Street. The store ran various promotions that included giving extraordinary, free items when customers made major purchases. (Macro Photography by Roger Schatz from Chicago Historical Society Photograph.)*

IRA MACKEVICH, RIGHT, WITH STORE MANAGER JAMES GOZZOLA, LATE 1950S. *Mackevich's Department Store's grew as several buildings adjacent to the main one at 712 West Maxwell, were acquired by the family. (Courtesy of Gene Mackevich.)*

GENE MACKEVICH, 2001. *(Courtesy Eshel Productions.)*

"We were expanding and expanding, but we weren't expanding in all different locations. We had all of our so-called productive eggs in the Maxwell Street basket. And, it worked out very, very well until finally, with the University of Illinois and the condemnations which started back in the late sixties, probably '68, '69, finally we were forced out in the early seventies."

Mackevich's Department Store was closed long before the final wrecking ball swung on Maxwell Street as the new century turned. Gene doesn't argue with the growth of the University of Illinois at Chicago, and understands what defines progress in urban development. However, he faults the way that drive for progress was accomplished.

"We had our first notification of eminent domain back as early as 1966 . . . we've been on a string, so to speak, like a puppet, for all of these years. That's insane. Absolutely ludicrous. Nobody should have to go through that. Nobody."

Gene Mackevich moved on into the financial world, becoming a very successful broker and financial advisor. His offices are high up in the Sears Tower where he can literally see the nearby area where Maxwell Street once thrived. The distance from the Sears Tower to Maxwell Street can also be measured in worlds, but there is a very definite linkage for Mackevich.

"I have my own theory, and I've told my children and my grandchildren, that today, in this modern society that we live in now, that I look at everything in the eyes of a merchant of Maxwell Street. And, I believe that the whole world is Maxwell Street.

"We learned to be able to understand other people. How they think, where they're coming from, what's important to them, and how to communicate at every single level. And, this was so important, because this gave us the knowledge and the education, although not formal, but the education to be able to get along with everybody. It means to put yourself in anybody else's shoes who's rational. And this is the gift that Maxwell Street gave me. It gave me the greatest education in the world. Now, you could say, well, I had a formal education in one of the top universities in the country. True. But, if you take the university formal education, and take the Maxwell Street, what I call day-to-day hard-knocks education, and the communication skills and all the things that went into learning what life was all about, and put A and B together, you end up with something that is priceless. You end up with something that nobody can take away from us. And this is the gift that I bring to my family. This is a gift that I bring to what professional success I may have."

Mackevich equates Maxwell Street to a path for achieving the American dream. He mentions some of the more prominent names that came from Maxwell Street to make his point; William S. Paley, CBS chairman; Arthur Goldberg, U.S. Supreme Court Justice and United Nations ambassador; Adm. Hyman Rickover, father of the nuclear submarine; and Jake Arvey, chairman of the Cook County Democratic Party.

"The fascination that I have with just these samples, a few names, whether they be local, business, professional or national, is that they all came from this immediate area. They all had their roots on Maxwell Street. They all had the same drive to accomplish the American dream. It almost sounds corny now, but looking at it from their perspective, coming from nothing, and working their way professionally and business-wise with only their guts and their mind and their wit. In my mind, it exemplifies what this whole area stands for.

"It doesn't matter if you're Italian, or Irish or the Greeks or African-American. It applies to everybody. But, you have to have the will, you have to have the desire. And the street seemed to bring out that benefit, that asset that people had and gave them the courage and the challenge . . . and the chutzpah."

"Everybody was bargaining. And, when they struck that bargain, it was a great feeling. The customer said, 'Boy, I really took those guys,' and we said, 'Boy, we took them.' And everybody walked away happy."

–Burt Weinstein

The name Weinstein was well-known on Maxwell Street. While there may have been someone named Weinstein selling shmattes off a push-cart, or more than ripe bananas off a table that also held a variety of rusted tools, the Weinsteins who operated a men's clothing store right on the northeast corner of Maxwell and Halsted probably came to many minds first when the name was mentioned from the 1930s onward. But that clothing business, actually started as a restaurant.

Burt and Jerry Weinstein's mother, Sarah Sidletsky, was born in New York City in 1909, shortly after her parents arrived from Poland. Sarah's father Philip and her mother, Anna, came to Chicago and settled in the Maxwell Street area.

Anna Sidletsky was an excellent cook. So the Sidletsky's opened a kosher restaurant a few doors east of the Maxwell and Halsted intersection, the true heart of the area. The Sidletsky's made a living.

"They didn't take money on Saturday," said Burt Weinstein. "The people just came back on Sunday and paid. And then, eventually, our maternal grandfather . . . and we don't know exactly how . . . got into the men's clothing business, and opened up a store on Maxwell Street. Probably in the basement where that restaurant really was."

While Philip Sidletsky built up his clothing business, Philip Weinstein and his two brothers, Jacob and Max, sold used clothing on Jefferson Street and Roosevelt Road, about half-a-mile from Maxwell Street. How the Sidletsky's and the Weinsteins got together isn't clear, but the Weinsteins eventually began working for Mr. Sidletsky. The young Philip Weinstein fell in love with Sidletsky's daughter, Sarah, and they married. When Sidletsky was hit hard by the Depression, Jacob Weinstein took over the business, called it Modern Clothing and operated it with his brothers.

Burt and Jerry Weinstein were two of the children of the Sarah Sidletsky–Philip Weinstein union, and they grew up working in the store.

"I was maybe six or seven years old," recalled Jerry. "I used to make the biggest pile of boxes. Little did I know that everybody made the same big pile of boxes but I was always told my pile of boxes was the best. It was exciting for me."

Jerry remembered how the clientele changed after World War II.

"It changed in the '50s with the migration of African-Americans to the north, they started coming down to the market more and more, and it changed. We didn't get that customer who used to come in from Iowa or Michigan on an early Sunday morning who would stop at the corner hot-dog stand to get a pork chop sandwich with the onions, and then the mustard, and they'd be coming in eating a sandwich and say, 'I want to get a suit.' and they're dripping with the mustard and the onions and everything over them. And the smell. I used to hate that smell in the morning."

"And our Dad knew them," said Burt. "Our dad would say, 'How are you? You're from Ames, Iowa?' My Dad and my uncles spoke a lot of languages, not fluently, they spoke them commercially, so that they could make a sale."

PHILIP SIDLETSKY, 1923. *He and his wife Anna came from Poland. Anna's cooking talents led them to open a Maxwell Street restaurant. Sidletsky opened a clothing store, probably in the basement where the restaurant was located. (Courtesy of Burt and Jerry Weinstein.)*

Of course, making the sale was everything. What Burt and Jerry learned from their father and uncles about not losing a sale is indicative of every successful merchant on Maxwell Street.

"There were never any prices on the clothing," said Burt. "There were tags and the tags would have the size. And in addition, there was a very convoluted code. The first number was the decade, like it was bought in 1950 . . . the number would be five. And the last number was the actual year. If it was bought in 1959, it would have five in the front and then nine in the back. And then there would be a designation for a month in there, and then there was the price that we paid for it, plus shipping and a little bit extra, divided by four."

"No, it was multiplied by two," corrected Jerry. "So if an item, let's say cost fifty dollars, the code would read approximately, let's say we bought it in August, so it would be 5-8-100-9."

"And from there," continued Burt, "you would begin your negotiations on the price, and they had no idea what the price of the merchandise was. They knew how much money they had in their pocket. I think the lesson that we both learned very, very early in our lives was to look at a person who came in and determine where in the store to take that person. Because if you took them to the hundred dollar suits, he would never buy the fifteen dollar suit because that's all he had in his pocket."

"So we had to look at the customer and figure out, 'Is he a hundred dollar suit person or a fifteen dollar suit person?'"

Jerry Weinstein agreed.

"You had to make a decision as to where you thought this person was going to fit, and sometimes you make the wrong decision. But, you learn from those mistakes about how to move someone around the store."

The brothers learned the intricacies from their elders.

"Our father and our uncles worked together," added Burt. "They would come up to the customer and greet them and they would say to us, 'Take him over there,' because they could really size them up and they would teach us. Dad, or our uncles would say,

PHILIP SIDLETSKY'S NATURALIZATION CERTIFICATE, ISSUED IN CHICAGO IN 1923. *(Courtesy of Burt and Jerry Weinstein.)*

'Look at his shoes,' for example. You'd see certain characteristics. If a man came in with his family, he was going to buy a suit for an occasion. If he came in with a bunch of guys, he was buying a suit for some dance and it was a one-time affair. So, I think that lesson, over a lot of years, is something that has helped me immeasurably. And I do it now sort of instinctively. And, I'm a lawyer, and I try lawsuits, and I look at people when I pick a jury. I think back at my Dad and my uncles, and how that lesson I learned there has just stayed with me.

"My Dad always told us," said Burt, "that you don't make money selling suits. You make money when you buy the suit. He said, 'If you can buy it right, then you sell it at a good price, give the customer a bargain and still make money.'

"The element of the bargain was what made Maxwell Street so vibrant."

Almost from the beginning of the Jewish experience on Maxwell Street, the area was called "Jew Town" by those who came looking for the bargains. Jews, of course, never liked the term, but in the expectations shoppers had of becoming part of the Maxwell Street experience, the bargains, the food, the crowds, the over-all atmosphere, "Jew Town" proved more a location than a slur. For the hard-working Jewish merchants, for those in stores

30

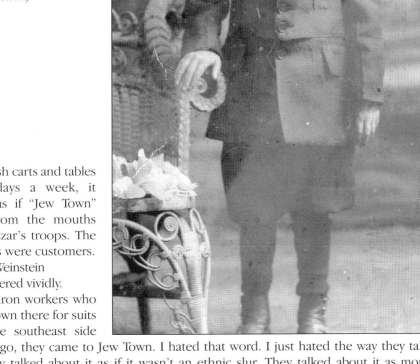

PHILIP WEINSTEIN, C. 1917. Weinstein and his brothers, Jacob and Max, began working at Philip Sidletsky's clothing store in the 1920s. Philip Weinstein married Sidletsky's daughter, and when the Great Depression hit, Weinstein took over the business and renamed it Weinstein's Modern Clothing. (Courtesy of Burt and Jerry Weinstein.)

or at push carts and tables seven days a week, it wasn't as if "Jew Town" came from the mouths of the Czar's troops. The speakers were customers.

Burt Weinstein remembered vividly.

"The iron workers who came down there for suits from the southeast side of Chicago, they came to Jew Town. I hated that word. I just hated the way they talked. And they talked about it as if it wasn't an ethnic slur. They talked about it as more of a description."

"It was a place," said Jerry. "It was a place to go."

"It was a place," agreed Burt. "And, I mean it was just something I can never . . . it would send a shudder through me all the time. And you just . . . you laughed about it and that was the end of it.

"People came in there, they wanted to buy a graduation suit for their kid, and it was a black woman with five or six kids, and she might have had ten dollars in her pocket. We had a lay-away system where a person could put five dollars down on a suit and we'd hold it for them, and they'd come in every week and make a payment on it, then finally they could take the suit out. Then you had all these Eastern European people.

"My Dad could speak a little Russian, spoke a little Polish, Ukrainian. It seemed they knew every language to speak, or at least they knew a language and could figure out what language the transaction would take place in."

PHILIP AND SARAH WEINSTEIN AND THEIR SONS, 1958. *Jerry is seated between his parents. Burt is standing on the left next to his brother, Hubert. The family operated Weinstein's Modern Clothing on the northeast corner of Maxwell and Halsted Streets. (Courtesy of Burt and Jerry Weinstein.)*

Today, Jerry Weinstein is a successful business consultant, and as his lawyer brother noted, the lessons of Maxwell Street merchandising go a long way.

"The lessons we learned as kids going down to Maxwell Street," stressed Burt, "were lessons of life about how to treat people, how people treated you, how to get along with people, how to treat them no matter what because you wanted to make a customer out of them with respect."

Jerry Weinstein underlined that statement.

"It was important to learn to listen, rather than do all the talking. Let them do the talking. Listen so you can learn what to do. And that's how I learned the best thing about dealing with people. And, I think that's probably the greatest lesson that we had there."

NEVER TAKE NO FOR AN ANSWER

Jordon Ross's parents, Joe and Lillian Ross, came from the Russia-Poland area in their late teens and settled in the Maxwell Street area with Joe's uncle, a butcher.

"My father worked as an apprentice butcher," said Jordon, "until he opened up his first and only butcher shop on Maxwell Street just west of Halsted.

"There was no such thing as a 40-hour week," Jordon explained. "My father was an observant Jew, a religious Jew, so he could not be open on Saturday, so Sunday was his biggest day. So Saturday night, as soon as the Sabbath was over, he went to the store to prepare the meat and worked maybe until twelve or one in the morning, and then by seven o'clock in the morning, he was back in the store to sell. And it taught us work ethics."

It was for the children. Most of the first generation Jewish merchants of Maxwell Street reasoned that way.

Ross remembers the thick sawdust on the floor, the chicken counter on one side, the meat counter on the other. The chickens were killed in the back of the store after customers made their selections. How the Ross's got the meat into the stores might seem outrageous today, but in the 1920s and '30s, you did what you had to do.

"I remember the one experience I had with my father, where, in those days, they didn't have delivery trucks. If he wanted meat to sell, he took the streetcar, the Halsted Street streetcar, which . . . we were at 13th (Street) in effect Maxwell Street. We took the streetcar south to 43rd Street on Halsted where the stockyards were. You went into the stockyards, you bought half a cow, you put some waxpaper on your back, you put the cow on the waxpaper, you got back on the streetcar, you rode down back north to 13th, to Maxwell Street, and you walked to the store and that's how you got delivery."

Ross worked in the store as a young boy and, when his father wasn't schlepping cows, listened carefully to the fatherly advice he heard repeatedly.

JOE ROSS'S MAXWELL STREET BUTCHER SHOP IN THE EARLY 1920s. Mr. Ross bought his beef at the Chicago Stockyards and carried it to the shop on the Halsted Street streetcar. (Courtesy of Jordon Ross.)

BUTCHER SHOP IN THE 1940S. *In the 1940s,, Joe Ross had a partner, Joe Brody. Chickens were sold and slaughtered on Brody's side of the shop. Ross sold meat products on the opposite side of the saw dust covered floor. Joe Ross made his living with his hands. He always told his son, Jordon, that he would make a living with his mind. (Courtesy of Jordon Ross.)*

"The one thing I continually remember my father telling me is, 'I have to do this. I earn my living with my hands. You're not going to. You're going to earn your living with your mind, and you're going to learn. You'll learn here, you'll work here, but you'll earn your living with your mind'."

It was a lesson well-learned. Jordon Ross took his Maxwell Street education and went on to become a very successful businessman and entrepreneur.

"Well, the first thing I learned was people, and how to deal with people. And from my point of view, and I think my personality was very much formulated there, in that, really, when someone says 'no' to you, for me, that was the beginning of a conversation, and surely the beginning of a negotiation."

Negotiation was always part of Maxwell Street. It was everywhere. You couldn't negotiate on price at Marshall Field's, but on Maxwell Street negotiation was integral to the shopping experience.

"When I was there it was basically Jewish merchants," Ross said. "The customers were Jews, were gentiles, blacks and anyone because that was the place to get a bargain. And you could buy anything there, from rusty nails to brand new shoes, brand new suits. I got my first suit there. My father took me to Weinstein Brothers down the street where I got my first suit. Who knew of shopping somewhere else? Marshall Fields was not a place for us to shop. Maxwell Street was where we bought things.

"I graduated Northwestern, and then got a Master's in accounting from Northwestern and then went on to DePaul Law School. The education meshed beautifully with the experiences, the work experiences I had through my life, and I got into various businesses. I invented the system for the television industry for residual payments and even today the company coordinating those payments, to my belief, is practically a monopoly, handling residual payments for the television industry. And today, I'm in the real estate finance business for government real estate. And, I have found that everything I've done, it comes from all the lessons of how to put together a deal, how to negotiate, it comes from understanding people."

Like so many others among the last Jewish generation from Maxwell Street, Jordon Ross offers deeply knowledgeable observations and opinions comparing present day professionals with his contemporaries.

"One of the jobs I had in front of, I don't remember which of the stores, was pulling in people, getting people to come in and buy things in the store. It just made an extrovert out of you, because if you weren't an extrovert, you couldn't be on Maxwell Street. And it just developed our personalities very young.

"I say those people who have learned to work in places like Maxwell Street like we did, and learned what business is really about, are so different than the MBAs that come out of the better schools. All they know how to do, from my experience, and I've had many of them work for me, is they know how to spout formulas that they memorized in school. Most of them have never had the experience that many of us had growing up in a place like Maxwell Street, learning what business was really about."

Those like Jordon Ross who grew up on Maxwell Street understand something else besides business.

"I'd say we all learned to help one another, in as much as everyone of us was scuffling, not so much us children, but our parents and grandparents who were scuffling for every dollar. They knew there was always someone coming into the store who didn't have, and as difficult as it may have been for everyone at times, there was always charity. Anybody in need who came to Maxwell Street knew that if they walked into a store, they wouldn't be turned away empty. As children we learned that that's part of life. You've got to give it back. You don't take it all."

JORDON ROSS, 2001.
". . . When someone says 'no' to you, for me, that was the beginning of a conversation, and surely, the beginning of a negotiation." (Courtesy Eshel Productions.)

SAM AND ISRAEL ACHLER, C. 1920. *Like Jordon Ross's father, Morris Achler, on the left, carried sides of beef on his shoulders while riding the streetcar from the stockyards. Morris's father, Sam, on the right, opened a butcher shop at 1312 S. Halsted before his son arrived in America. Less than five-feet tall, Morris was smaller than most of the sides of beef he carried. His real name was Israel Achler, but he forever took the identity of his brother, a Russian soldier killed in World War I, because the real Morris Achler had proper papers for immigrating. (Courtesy of Mark Achler, Morris's grandson.)*

2.

Aim Low

SMOKEY JOE'S

"Like the shopping malls of today, Maxwell Street also had anchors: Turner Brothers, Mackevich, etc. But the most famous, notorious of these, depending on one's experiences, was Smokey Joe's, which was a most amazing mix of sartorial splendor. Every brand and style of suit, jacket, shirt, shoes, coats one could imagine, or so it seemed. And the salesmen, especially a guy named Morry, made you really imagine! When you tried on any of Morry's inventory, he had a way of making you feel that you were the equal of the great stars of the time—Frank Sinatra, Dean Martin, Clark Gable, Tyrone Power."
*   –Tony Fontana*

Esther Weinstein Bublick's father Jacob shot himself in the leg to avoid service in the Russian Army. He did it, she said, because he observed kashruth laws, (keeping a kosher home). "Being Jewish and kosher, he would have to give up religion," Ms. Bublick recounted. She didn't mention that draftees in Russia were often committed to 25 years of service. Maybe that fact also entered into Jacob Weinstein's decision to shoot himself. But whatever the reason, his method worked. He wound up in Chicago around 1912. First Jacob Weinstein was a peddler, then a jobber selling merchandise to Maxwell Street vendors, and eventually operated his own clothing store, the same Modern Clothing business at 744 Maxwell Street noted in the earlier story, "Learning to Listen." (Esther's cousins are Jerry and Burt Weinstein.)

Esther Weinstein met Max Bublick in that store when they were both teenagers. Her father gave his father, Joe Bublick, a concession space in the store.

"He gave my dad a room...well, a table about the size of a dining room table," Max remembered. "In those days, they were selling suits . . . two pair of pants suits for twenty-two dollars. . . . In order to get a better break, customers would buy it with one pair of pants. So my dad bought the extra pants, we put it on the table, and started out doing business selling pants."

"Our parents sacrificed. They worked hard," Esther said passionately. "They worked from early in the morning, every night until nine o'clock. Sundays . . . they didn't have days off. And that's their sacrifice. They didn't have enough time to spend with their children. My mother was a stay-at-home mother. But Max's mother worked all the time with the sewing and stuff like that. And it must have been very hard, but it was a natural thing for them to do, because that's what they wanted, and they wanted the best for us."

The Maxwell Street roots that Esther's family established led to a succession of successful businesses. Her late brother and her brother-in-law opened Irv's, a well-known Chicago area men's clothing chain that remains in business.

And that pants table Max's father started with, expanded into a very successful clothing operation called Smokey Joe's. The name evolved from wholly American illogic. Joe Bublick

JOSEPH AND ESTHER BUBLICK WITH THEIR CHILDREN, 1935. *Morry is pictured on the left, with Roz and Max. Joe began what would evolve into Smokey Joe's when Esther Weinstein's father leased him a concession stand on Maxwell Street.*

never smoked, so someone called him "Smokey Joe."

Just before World War II, Max was helping to run the business after school.

"I went to work, so my dad was able to go to the various jobbers on Roosevelt Road and buy merchandise, and we would get that merchandise, and then sell it over the weekend, and Monday they would line up. We didn't have a checking account. And my dad would give this guy fifty bucks, another guy seventy-five, depending on how much he owed him, and that's the way the business was going."

After Max finished college with an accounting degree, Smokey Joe's finally opened a checking account. They needed it. Business was very good.

"I remember how we had to fight, because the big retailers downtown didn't want any retailers doing business on Sunday," Max said. "A few of the storekeepers closed on Saturday because it was the Jewish Sabbath, but Sunday was the big day. So the merchants on Maxwell Street raised money and got lawyers to fight down in Springfield. And finally, we won the fight and were able to stay open on Sunday. But, now everybody is open on Sunday. That's their big day."

Smokey Joe's truly was a trend-setting business.

"My brother Morry was a character," said Max. "He was known throughout the industry. He designed the Zoot Suit."

"A lot of the black entertainers came to have their uniforms or suits, jazzy-looking suits, made at Smokey Joe's," said Esther.

"We were the highest style in the country," said Max. "We met with three or four other stylists from New York, and Cleveland. We'd have a meeting maybe once a year, but we

ESTHER WEINSTEIN AND MAX BUBLICK ON THEIR WEDDING DAY, MARCH 23, 1945. Max's father owned Smokey Joe's clothing store. Esther and Max knew each other from Maxwell Street. On Navy leave during World War II, she saw Max in Washington, D.C. when he was on leave from Iceland. She was engaged to the son of another Maxwell Street merchant at the time, but broke the engagement and married Max. (Courtesy of Esther and Max Bublick.)

were the highest style. That was my brother, not my doing. My brother was the one who designed the clothes, 'cuz he liked to wear that type of clothes."

At the beginning of their music careers, Michael Jackson and the Jackson Five came from their Gary, Indiana home to have their costumes made at Smokey Joe's. Michael Jackson was very young.

"When he was a little boy," said Max.

"They made uniforms for them," added Esther.

"But we didn't have any boys' suits that would match the men's suits," said Max.

"So they cut down the men's suit," said Esther.

"I told the salesman to make the sale. Cut down the suit and remake it whatever it is. I was able to make the suits smaller, and make a suit bigger than it was. If a guy needed a 50 and we had a 46, I would tell my tailor how to do the thing. I'd cut up a pair of pants and insert the V or something. In order to sell to a group, 'cuz that's what we sold a lot of," added Max.

"He kept the books," Esther made clear with a giggle.

"I kept the books. I kept us in business," echoed Max, laughing.

Esther and Max married in March of 1945. He was in the Army, stationed in Iceland as a radio operator. Esther had joined the Waves and was assigned to the Navy Bureau of Personnel in Washington. She was engaged to the son of a Maxwell Street luggage store owner, but she and Max had exchanged letters. On furlough in the nation's capitol, Max called. "He called me from the airport and asked if I'd meet him for lunch. And I did. And evidently, I smelled better than the Icelandic women who all stunk from fish."

"We got engaged," laughed Max.

"And he asked me to marry him," said Esther. She gave her engagement ring back to her other fiancé.

"I remember when I was younger," said Max. "If I had to go buy something, I'd go to Maxwell Street. I didn't take money in my pocket. I'd go to Mages Sporting Goods Store. If I needed a pair of gym shoes, I'd get the shoes. I'd say, 'My dad will pay.' It was family. It

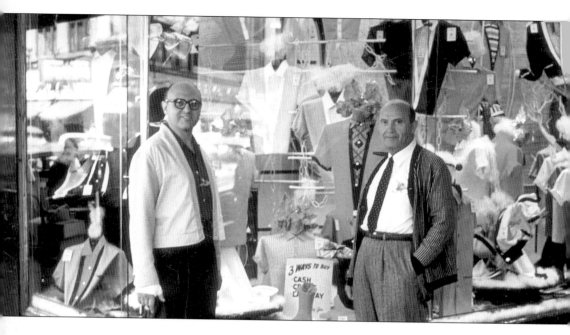

MAX, LEFT, AND HIS FATHER JOE BUBLICK IN FRONT OF SMOKEY JOE'S ON HALSTED STREET. *The store was a trend setter, designing many of the men's fashions that other stores would copy. If you wanted "cool," Smokey Joe's was where you shopped. Max credits his brother Morry with designing the "Zoot Suit." "I kept the books, I kept us in business," said Max. (Courtesy of Esther and Max Bublick.)*

was really like a small. . . . I can only explain . . . it was like a small town. A small shtetl."

"We went to a jeweler to get my engagement ring," Esther said, "and Max said, 'My dad will pay,' 'cuz he had no money."

The Bublick's have three daughters. All of them worked in Smokey Joe's.

"I remember all my daughters worked," said Max. "And they all worked at some time as a cashier. And it was very important, because I knew, just from being a cashier and meeting these people, if things got really tough, they can always get a job."

"Our daughter Tracey," Max went on, "used to come down on Saturday and Sunday. She remembers when she was five years old. I gave her a job: 'Count how many shirts are in this liner. Do this.' And when she found out they were ripping down Maxwell Street, I had to take her down and she had to look at the buildings."

Tracey remembered her last look at the street.

"I remember going to see Maxwell Street when they were beginning the tear down," she wrote. "I walked along the street and found Smokey Joe's written in the tile of the entrance way to the store. It was still there all these years later. I cried. It's my family . . . our history in those tiles. I wish it was still standing so I could bring my children to see. It is still a warm feeling when you run into people who also have family from Maxwell Street. All these years later it still has that same old world family feel . . . a connection.

"I have the stories to hold onto, the days I spent working at the store, the people who came in as regulars every weekend for a new "going out" outfit. My father was in his prime then. He truly found happiness and fulfillment at Smokey Joe's. He loved the customers, the employees, the high fashion grind was in his blood. Smokey Joe's was my father's fourth child."

SHARPSHOOTER

Russian-Jewish men must have been very good marksmen. Many didn't miss when aiming at their feet in an effort to avoid serving in the Czar's army. Mischa Korczemski was already in the Russian Army when he shot himself in his left leg, just above the ankle. According to his daughter, Harriet Karm Berman, Mischa's plan was to recuperate at home and then desert.

Mrs. Berman's story, "The Street," was first published in the Chicago Jewish Historical Society's quarterly journal, *Chicago Jewish History*, in the spring of 2002. She wrote that her father's painful, but obviously determined plot worked. With the help of other family members who had preceded them to Chicago, Mischa, and apparently most of the Korczemskis, wound up working on Maxwell Street.

MARTIN KARM. *Karm is seen here at the bottom of the stairway, when he was selling men's clothes on Maxwell Street. Karm shot himself in the foot to escape the Russian Army, deserted the Czar's troops, and made his way to Chicago. (Courtesy of Harriet Karm Berman.)*

In the United States, the family name became Karm, and Mischa became Martin. Martin Karm met Rose Levin in an English class at the Jewish People's Institute. Both were twenty years old when they married.

"Shortly after, their first child, my brother Jerry was born," Harriet Berman wrote, "Mischa and Rose relocated to Bloomington and optimistically opened a Jewish deli. Alas, this was an idea before its time. In the late 1920s, Bloomington, Illinois, site of the state teachers' college, was not yet ready for lox, bagels, and hot corned beef sandwiches.

"They returned to Chicago and Mischa began working on Maxwell Street again, as a salesman for Taxman & Dlugatch Clothiers.

"After some years, Mischa and a fellow salesman, Morris 'Buby' Zolt, opened a small men's wear store, Martin's Clothes at 716 Maxwell Street. There were no visible prices on the garments they sold. Prices were determined by a complicated secret code written on each tag, and successful sales were the result of hard bargaining."

Eventually, Martin Karm would start another clothing business, Clinton Clothiers, at Roosevelt Road and Clinton Street. While Mrs. Berman says she didn't work in her father's stores, she remembers vividly, the atmosphere of the area.

"There was genial camaraderie despite being competitors. On Sundays, the Street was mobbed with bargain-hunting shoppers. Street musicians abounded. Mahalia Jackson, the great gospel singer, frequently performed on the corner of Maxwell and Halsted.

"My brothers helped out at the store on weekends, but I wasn't allowed to come along, probably because I was a girl. The exclusion didn't bother me much because I was terrified of the gypsies, who, from their street level windows, beckoned with forefinger to passing youngsters."

As a college student, Harriet Berman once read an editorial in the *Daily Illini*, the student newspaper at the University of Illinois, that charged Maxwell Street merchants with cheating customers and, "living in the lap of luxury."

"I blasted off a letter to the editor, refuting his words. When my letter appeared in the paper several days later, I felt satisfied that my father and the other hardworking Maxwell Street vendors had been vindicated. Upon my next visit home, my father, eyes twinkling, placed both issues of the *Daily Illini* in front of me. 'Where did you get those?' I sputtered in amazement. He smiled a slow, all-knowing smile and said, 'Oh, the Street has its sources. Nothing escapes us. The editor's own grandfather has a store on the Street.'"

STRATEGY AND TACTICS

Y ou could always find second-hand items on Maxwell Street.
Even bakeries had what you might consider second-hand merchandise. The Chicago Bargain Bakery was the perfect name for Sam Robin's business on Maxwell Street. All the goods in the bakery were one-day-old. Nothing was baked in the store. The bakery goods were purchased from larger bakeries. The bakery did a brisk business. Sam Robin's son, Paul remembers taking the streetcar from his home in Humboldt Park on the north side of Chicago to work with his father.

Paul Robin also was in the rag trade, working for a clothier called B. Sher & Son, located on Roosevelt Road. There he learned the quintessential strategy of selling. He learned the tactics for expanding a sale so that a customer never left with just one item.

"My boss always said, if you sell a tie, sell a shirt. If you sell a shirt and a tie, sell him cufflinks. If you sell him a shirt, a tie, and cufflinks, don't let him leave without a tie clasp."

SAM ROBIN IN HIS SECOND-HAND BAKERY SHOP ON MAXWELL STREET, 1930s. His son, Paul worked in the store, and later was a clothing salesman who learned the art of making sure customers didn't leave without buying an array of merchandise. (Courtesy of Paul Robin.)

Maxwell Street University Alumni

"You don't learn how to make money in school. But, on Maxwell Street, yes. My parents worked hard. My mother worked with my father and it was a burden for them to send me to college, me and my sister to college. And I worked all through school. I always worked. I went to work for my father on Maxwell Street, then I worked at an A & P as a stock boy. I worked nights, I worked days, I delivered papers, sold magazines, the Saturday Evening Post *from hotel to hotel and room to room, lobby to lobby. I worked at Ashkenosh up on Morris Avenue as a soda jerk. I did it all. I did it all. And learned at everyone of them. But Maxwell Street was the best. That was the best. Nothing like it."*

–Sheldon Good

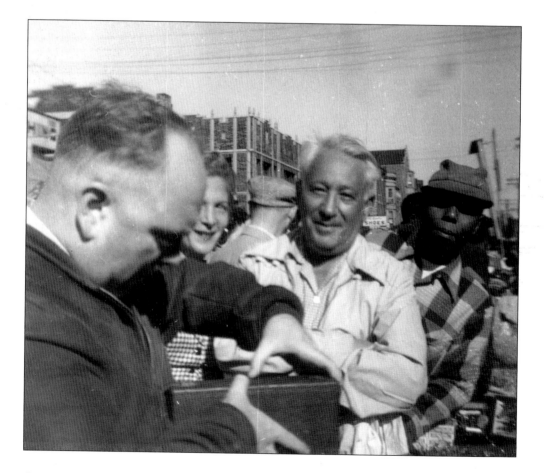

Sylvia and Joseph Good with a Customer on Maxwell Street, 1944. *The man to Good's left and behind, worked for him. He is Clayton Taylor, now 83-years old and living in Georgia. (Courtesy of Sheldon Good and Ferne Stone.)*

***Litman Schwartz and His Wife Tille,
c. 1920.*** *Sheldon Good and Ferne Stone's
maternal grandfather was Litman Schwartz.
Schwartz ran a butcher shop at 707 West
Maxwell Street. He leased a space in front of the
shop to Joseph Good who began selling hard-to-
find merchandise during World War II. (Courtesy
of Sheldon Good and Ferne Stone.)*

If Maxwell Street were a blood type, it would be on Sheldon Good's medical chart because Maxwell Street runs through his veins.

Sheldon Good operates one of the most successful real estate businesses in America. He has been president of the 7,000 member Chicago Association of Realtors, and president of the Commercial Investment Division of the National Association of Realtors. He was the first Jewish person to hold the office of president of the International Real Estate Federation. Of the hundreds of thousands of University of Illinois graduates, Sheldon Good was named one of the few hundred most outstanding alumni. The list of honors bestowed on him is very long and impressive.

Sheldon Good is a salesman. He learned how to sell when he hawked watches worn all the way up his arm on Maxwell Street.

"My father had me going up and down the street selling, selling whatever I could sell. So he gave me four or five watches. I put the watches on my arm, I'd walk with a long-sleeved shirt on a Sunday morning. . . . I'll never forget . . . and all these fancy, rich people looking for bargains would come down to Jew Town to find something. I would walk up and I'd say, 'Hey, mister, wanna buy a hot watch cheap?' Well, the watches weren't hot at all, my father had got them from another business he ran on west Madison Street. And I'd sell a watch for twelve dollars or eight dollars or ten dollars, or whatever it was, and I used to do the same thing with sunglasses."

Like so many others on Maxwell Street, Good learned quickly that when a would-be buyer said, "no," it really was the start of a selling opportunity . . . a negotiation.

"I learned how to sell on Maxwell Street, I really did. When that first fella I gave an elbow to, some of 'em just ran away from me. They were afraid of me. They thought I was a pickpocket or something. But, most of 'em, and I was a young boy, most of 'em would look at me and when they looked at me they'd take a look at my arm, I knew I had 'em. I says, 'You know, I'm on your side. I'll give you a good price, a really good. . . .' and I'd suck 'em right in."

45

SHELDON GOOD AND HIS SISTER FERNE. *In the 1940s, Sheldon and Ferne would help their father sell clothing and watches on Maxwell Street. Their grandfather ran a Kosher butcher shop and their father would set up a stand in front at 707 West Maxwell. (Courtesy of Sheldon Good and Ferne Stone.)*

Below: **FERNE STONE AND HER BROTHER, SHELDON GOOD, 2001.**

Good's family came to Maxwell Street from Poland and Romania. His maternal grandfather had a butcher shop at 707 West Maxwell. His mother was born above the store. His father came to America as a young boy, always telling how when the ship that brought the family from Europe passed the Statue of Liberty, everyone fell to their knees and kissed the deck.

Sheldon was born in 1933. His sister, Ferne Stone, is younger. Being on Maxwell Street and helping their father defines much of their lives. As far back as they can remember, they helped their father operate a table full of everything, set up on Sundays in front of the grandfather's butcher shop.

"Most of what was for sale on the table came from my father's general merchandise business on west Madison Street," Sheldon said. "During World War II, a lot of the merchandise that my father had in the store became very valuable. Where my father's store was, was really the area where a lot of the gandies, or railroad workers lived in the flophouses up and down west Madison Street when they weren't working. When they went on their jobs, they would check their clothes with my father for a month or two or three. I think he charged them fifty cents a month. And some of them came back, and some of them didn't come back. So, my father had all this stuff. Well, he started going through their stuff maybe two, three years later. It was just a pile of everything. New stuff, used stuff."

Good's mother suggested her husband take the unclaimed "stuff," and sell it on Maxwell Street. For Ferne Stone, those Sundays with her father remain some of her favorite memories.

"We would first go to his store on Madison and Des Plaines," she remembers. "He would take the back seat out of the car, and fill up the back of the car with tools and eyeglasses. He was an optometrist on the side, and he would test eyes."

"The headlines. The headlines!" remembered Sheldon.

"War Is Declared!" said Ferne.

"Yeah, right," said Sheldon.

"Or, Peace, VJ Day," said Ferne.

"That's how he'd check their eyes. He'd give 'em a newspaper to read. 'See if you can see.' It was all headlines. The paper was all headlines," remembered Sheldon.

"He was a wonderful, wonderful man. Loving man, caring," said Ferne. "And then you had to get there very early, because if you didn't, the space would close up where your pushcart went. And even though you paid the market master, somebody else, if they were there earlier than you were, came in and spread out a little more than they did the week before. So we got there very early, and I would stack the reading glasses, and then I was a watcher. I would watch."

"To make sure nobody would steal anything," Sheldon said with a laugh.

That table out front of the butcher shop at 707 West Maxwell and the commerce coming from it was, for Sheldon and Ferne, a window ledge with a panorama that showed them how to prevail and who they really were.

"We got motivated," said Sheldon.

"Got motivated, but we also saw a different side of life than we lived, and I think because of that, we became more aware of Jewish life, and Jewish giving and helping, helping others," said Ferne.

Ferne Stone never lost that motivation. She has been active in numerous fund-raising projects for Jewish organizations. She and her husband, Howard Stone, when he was chairman of the Jewish United Fund (JUF) in Chicago, led the successful efforts to raise 50 million dollars for the 1990–1991 general campaign and another 30 million for the campaign to help Jews leave Russia and immigrate to Israel.

"The reason I bring it up," said Ferne, is that we were brought up respecting Judaism, and knowing that there are those who are poor and don't have what we have. And I think part of it is from our experience and seeing a different side of life that I don't . . . that we didn't really feel. And wouldn't have felt had we not had the experience of Maxwell Street."

Sheldon Good summarized his Maxwell Street motivations and how it led to his extraordinary successes.

"Well, I think we're a product of our environment, and of course, Maxwell Street was a 20-year part of my environment. I went to Maxwell Street as many years as I went to school.

JOSEPH AND SYLVIA GOOD WITH THEIR CHILDREN. *The family is pictured here in 1946 at the Belden-Stratford Hotel celebrating Sheldon's Bar Mitzvah. (Courtesy of Sheldon Good and Ferne Stone.)*

We were business people. I mean, even though we were selling for nickels, we were in business. We had a product to sell, we had to get it to the buyer. Who is going to buy it? How are we going to negotiate with them and get them to take ours over somebody else's. And that's the same thing I do today. The exact same thing. I've got to sell somebody on why they should do business with me and why I should sell it to them, and I did it door-to-door the same way. Out on the street, door-to-door.

"I learned how to meet people, how to deal with people. I saw the market in its rawest form. Here's what I've got. Here's what I'm offering. How much will you pay for it? It was merchandising in its rawest form. In fact, all those flea markets you see today, all the discount stores and shopping stores that are discounters today, all copied off those Jewish markets that were done on Maxwell Street. Same thing. Same idea."

Pots and pans were everywhere in the Maxwell Street market. There were fine quality, new pots and pans, and many that had seen too many stoves. Pots and pans hung from peddlers' carts that also featured crystal chandeliers and a reconditioned pair of long-johns. In the first years of the 20th century such inventories were not unusual.

After Henry Mages came from Romania with his wife and family, he made a few extra dollars on Maxwell Street selling pots and pans. But, not for long.

"My grandfather was a tailor," Larry Mages, son of Morrie Mages recalled, ". . . but my

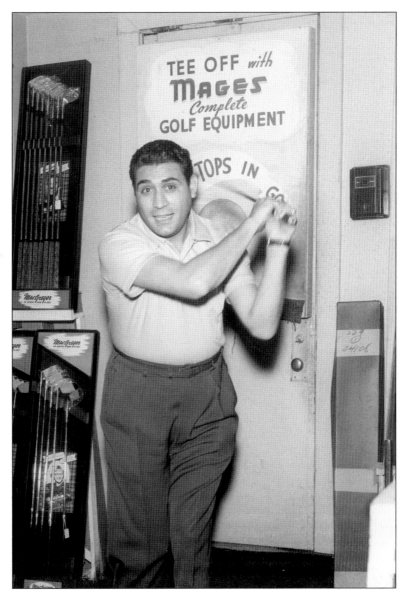

MORRIE MAGES IN THE 1950s. His grandfather started the sporting goods business on Maxwell Street. Morrie took the name Mages to television in memorable, live, and long commercials that led to sell-outs of featured items the next day. (Courtesy of the Mages Family.)

grandmother insisted that he'd bring home a little extra money. And so, on weekends, he would get a pushcart and he would just buy whatever merchandise he could and sell it off the cart. He started buying a lot of pots and pans, and in one odd lot that he bought there were some baseball gloves. And the story was that the baseball gloves sold faster than the pots and pans. He felt he had something, so from that point on, he just looked for a product, baseball gloves and products in the sporting goods field, and eventually that's all he did, and wound up owning a store down there."

Henry Mages sold so many baseball gloves he opened a sporting goods store at 835 Maxwell Street. Then he opened a second sporting goods store at 638 Maxwell Street.

Would this become the American dream?

Absolutely, but with an occasional nightmare.

That odd lot of baseball gloves proved the beginning of a Chicago retailing institution and Morrie Mages, one of Henry's sons, was the man Chicagoans would always identify with the name Mages.

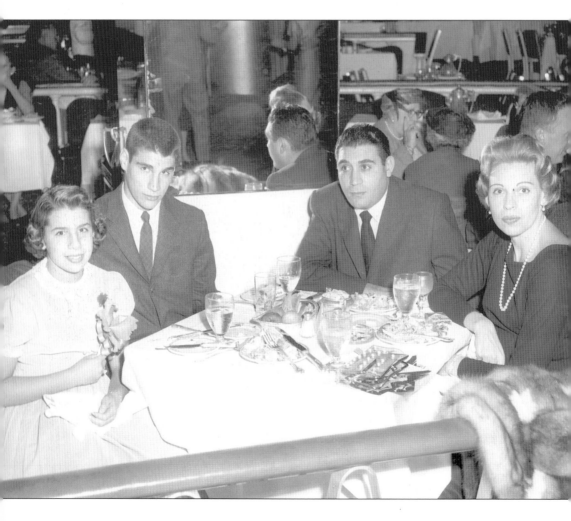

MORRIE AND SHIRLEE MAGES WITH THEIR CHILDREN, LILI ANN AND LARRY, 1950s. (Courtesy of the Mages Family.)

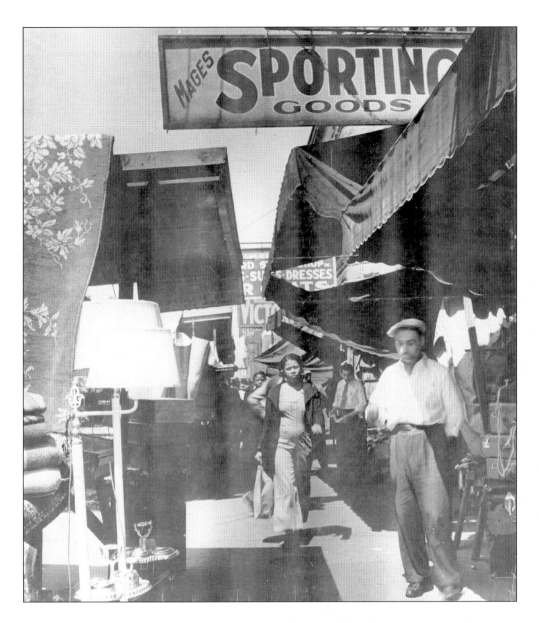

MAGES SPORTING GOODS STORES ON MAXWELL STREET, 1940. *Henry Mages started the business selling a few baseball gloves he found stuffed in an odd lot of pots and pans. Mages Sporting Goods would grow to a 14 store, publicly traded chain before the business went bankrupt. (Courtesy of Lili Ann Mages Zisook.)*

By the time the company was Mages Sporting goods, it was, at its peak in the 1950s, owner of 14 sporting goods stores, an auto dealership, a boating sales center, and two bowling alleys.

"They were listed on the American Stock Exchange," said Larry Mages. "They went public in 1956. As a matter of fact, I still have a baseball signed by Mickey Mantle, who bought the first 100 shares of stock."

Morrie Mages certainly brought the Maxwell Street aura to television. Television in the 1950s was live. There was no video tape until 1956. On WGN-TV in Chicago, Morrie Mages advertised his business in memorable, live commercials along with Jack Brickhouse, who, at the time, was both the Cubs and White Sox television play-by-play announcer and is enshrined in the broadcaster's section of the Baseball Hall of Fame. Brickhouse played the straight man and Morrie carried on about the, "Moment of Madness" sales at Mages Sporting Goods.

"You're talking back in about 1950, and again, I'm 10-years old," recalled Larry. "I remember going down to the studio with him. It was all done at WGN. And I mean, I became a model then. I mean, I could model jackets. I had half my high school and grammar school class going down there modeling sporting goods, so I was a big celebrity then. But it made my father all over Chicago.

"They had movies, they had game shows, commercials . . . my father and Jack Brickhouse . . . their commercials could last 35 minutes, just talking back and forth about what they did during the day, or what they planned on doing after the show was over."

The ratings for those Mages-sponsored programs and the extraordinary Mages commercials had to be significant. There was no doubt Chicago and suburbs were tuned in. Morrie's nephew, Marty Mages, remembered what it was like in the Mages stores the day after Morrie's "Moment of Madness" commercials had been telecast.

"You had to be there yourself to really see it. When Morrie was on Thursday night television they would put a bowling ball, a bag, and shoes for $24.99. That was the featured item. The next day Brunswick Company themselves couldn't make us enough bowling balls to take care of everybody, we were so busy."

Eventually, of course, television changed, the world changed, and the success of the Mages empire ran into some wicked curve balls. Strike three brought bankruptcy. But the game wasn't over yet. With his Maxwell Street savvy, Morrie Mages started over again.

At his daughter Lili Ann's suggestion, Mages started selling skis. Larry, an attorney, came into the business to help. The skis sold out. Mages bought more. The skis sold out again. Eventually, the revitalized Mages Sports had only one store. But, what a store! All eight floors of a huge building at the intersection of LaSalle and Ontario Streets were filled with sporting goods.

"The store we had on LaSalle Street was like a miniature Maxwell Street to my father," said Larry. "We had sidewalk sales on LaSalle Street. I mean, this was downtown Chicago. Nobody did that kind of stuff. We put tables out. You couldn't walk into our store without . . . we didn't have pushcarts . . . but we had tables loaded with merchandise. You could not walk into the store without bumping into these tables. He merchandised as if he lived his whole life on Maxwell Street."

MORRIE MAGES' SKI SALES. *Ski sales took Mages out of bankruptcy and led him once again to becoming Chicago's sporting goods business leader. Before selling out to a large chain, the Mages family operated a huge, eight-story high-rise store at LaSalle and Ontario Streets. (Courtesy of the Mages Family.)*

The Mages family wasn't the only sporting goods business on Maxwell Street.

Maurice Olshansky opened Maurice Sporting Goods at 810 West Maxwell in 1921. He had left Russia for a number of reasons, one of which was the specter of being drafted into the Red Army.

After working in a pickle business, and then selling musical instruments, Olshansky found his calling on Maxwell Street. His store was but a little, windowless room, 20 by 25 feet, a potbelly stove and a toilet. Olshansky's daughter, Fay Katlin said the store was, ". . . my home away from home, . . . my cave of comfort."

"I laugh out loud when I think about my father having a sporting goods store. I'm sure when he arrived in this country in 1921 he had never seen a baseball or a baseball bat, a football, a tennis racket, or a basketball . . . Of course," Ms. Katlin remembers, "he did get into the business in a roundabout way. My mother, like most Eastern European women, learned to knit, crochet, and sew as a young girl. Being an excellent seamstress, she made uniforms for the local school bands and orchestras, while my father sold them musical instruments. The school athletic departments liked the uniforms my mother made and ordered some uniforms for their teams."

Maurice Olshansky wasn't blind. He was selling more uniforms than flutes. He saw how the sports uniforms could lead to his selling sports equipment. The switch-over from mandolins to medicine balls wasn't long in coming. The business was the only means of support for Olshansky, his wife, his parents, one daughter, and two sons.

"In the store, I helped fold and sort merchandise, opened boxes, learned to count, add and subtract in English, Yiddish, and Russian," Fay Katlin said.

For Ms. Katlin, Maxwell Street was, and remains a very special world.

"Many of the people I know spent their childhood playing in their backyards or the local parks. I spent most of mine in the 'Casbah.' No, not the one we remember in the movie, *Casablanca,* but the one in Chicago, Maxwell Street. My 'Casbah' was a business community straight out of the Arabian nights with stores, stands, pushcarts, wagons, and boxes, jumbled together on the west side of the city. Within its boundries you could buy almost anything you wanted or needed from people with accents originating all over the world. They often brought

MAURICE OLSHANSKY. *Maurice Olshansky escaped service in the Red Army and opened a sporting goods store on Maxwell Street in 1921. (Courtesy of Fay Katlin.)*

their native dress and scents with them, blending and creating exotic sights and aromas, enticing one into the bosom of the market.

"On weekends, huge crowds gathered and I could barely squeeze through the mass of vendors and customers. Excitement mounted that couldn't be experienced anywhere else in the world. The Grand Bazaar in Turkey, the famous markets in Egypt, Mexico, and the one I love in the Old City of Jerusalem, can't compare with the diversity, color, scent, or visual delights of Maxwell Street."

When Fay would leave her father's sporting goods store she'd always go and find some of the extraordinary people of Maxwell Street who would, unknowingly to her at the time, shape her life.

"Every morning, Ray Bloom stood in front of my father's store, his black eyes darting in every direction, framed by thick eyelashes wet from snow in the winter and wet from perspiration in the summer, anxiously awaiting the arrival of my father. When and where Ray came from I have no idea but he was part of my life from my earliest memories. I don't even know the origin of his relationship with my father. I have a sense like a squatter. Ray wandered into the store one day, my father sent a kind wave his way, Ray put his merchandise down and stayed. Ray was there because he sold pants. In this store crowded with merchandise, Ray was allotted a section on top of one of the showcases to display his pants. He spent his time endlessly counting his pants. If I looked over to the corner of the store, I could see his mass of unruly, wavy, directionless hair atop his hunched-back body, covered in his all-season black wool coat, bent over his pants. The rest of the time he spent

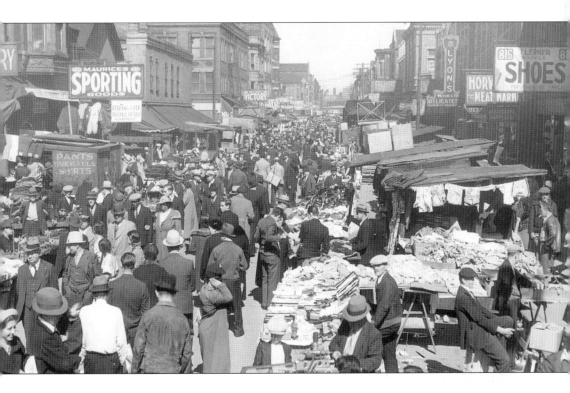

MAURICE'S SPORTING GOODS STORE, 1930s. Located in the 800 block of west Maxwell Street, just west of Halsted, Maurice's Sporting Goods Store can be seen here in the upper left. (From the David R. Phillips Collection.)

hours talking to himself, his soft voice, like elevator music, humming in the background of our busy day. At midday, he would pull out his brown, smaltz herring stained bag and begin offering everyone, particularly me, some of its contents.

"As quiet and soft-spoken as Ray was, every once-in-a-while, like a shot of lighting, he would become extremely agitated and start shouting, 'The bum. The bum is here.' His eyes would grow wider, his whole body would twitch violently while he wrapped his arms around his head to protect himself from the 'bum.' Everyone present directed their attention toward Ray, as if a spotlight had been focused on him. There was nothing that precipitated his arousal, it just came out of nowhere, but it came fast and furiously. 'Oy, Oy, the bum is here,' his voice desperately pleading for protection. 'The bum, the bum.' He would run and hide behind the counter, warning us, 'Be careful of the bum,. Hide! Hide!' He would crouch way down, his hands protecting his head, as if he were expecting to be beaten. My pudgy, bald father, who looked more like a pumpkin than a rescue hero, would immediately rush to Ray's side, patting his back and in a quiet voice assure him everything would be all right and he would protect Ray.

" 'Allis vet zon geet' . . . Everything will be O.K., I'll protect you.

"After a while, Ray would calm down, stop screaming, reassure my father he was all right and go back to counting his pants. Everyone would go back to whatever they had been doing before his outburst. All would return to normal. I never saw the 'bum' and never thought to ask my father or mother if they saw him. They seemed to handle the situation without any undue angst, so I did too.

"Years later, as an adult social worker, I realized Ray was a paranoid schizophrenic and that my father taught me my first social work techniques: When you are with an agitated person, speak softly, slowly and soothe.

"Where did my father learn these behaviors? Was he innately a kind gentle person, who naturally soothed others? Being loved by my father meant being unconditionally accepted.

"As I watched my father care for Ray, and Ray, in turn care for me, I believed I learned how to care for others."

Fay called Maxwell Street her, "Magic Kingdom."

"Sometimes I liked to sit on the stand in front of my father's store and just watch the people walk by. I pretended that the gypsy women in their dresses of rusty red satin and grasshopper green, thick cotton, patchwork pieces of fabric, were princesses from another country. I imagined the men in torn shirts and tattered pants had just jumped off railroad cars. The men wearing spiffy suits and ties I was sure were presidents of the local banks. Some of the clergy of various denominations in their black frocks frightened me. Then, there were days when I just counted the different hats I saw. There was such an abundance of baseball caps, sun bonnets, fedoras, skull caps, berets, Irish caps, and scarves. It was truly a United Nations of head coverings."

There was the jewelry repair man, a dwarf from Germany. He wasn't Jewish but welcomed Fay to his little business and let her sit on a stool next to him as he repaired wrist watches and clocks. She always thought of the watchmaker when she was older and understood the evil of Nazi Germany. She thought that her little German friend, because he was a dwarf, probably would have been exterminated by Hitler.

Fay thought of Maxwell Street, her father's store and her American life when she visited the Auschwitz concentration camp in 1986 on a cold, freezing Polish day.

"The snow and wind howled through the camp turning my tears to ice as they ran down my face. Remembering that stove in my father's store was enough to help warm me."

3.

Pullology
THE PULLERS

"Maxwell Street could be a thriving landmark, complete with kiosks and stands and stores (with the dubious charms of their 'pullers,' that sometimes overly aggressive sales force, on the sidewalk). 'In the old days,' Mike Royko once wrote, 'they didn't stand outside and coax you into the store. They hauled you in if you weren't big enough to resist. The only reasons they stopped was because an ordinance was passed prohibiting the kidnapping of customers.' "

–Ira Berkow
Excerpt from address at the University of Iowa, February, 1995.
(Ira Berkow of the *New York Times*
is author of *Maxwell Street: Survival in a Bazaar*,
Garden City: Doubleday & Co. 1977.)

The pullers on Maxwell Street were like carnival barkers. They were like the sirens of Greek mythology that drew victims to an unwanted fate. A good puller on Maxwell Street could get you to buy a hundred-dollar suit when what you really wanted was a flashlight.

Jacob Pomeranz is a labor attorney in Chicago with the firm of Cornfield and Feldman. But, on Maxwell Street he was a puller. For him, the puller's job was a classroom long before torts seminars, contract negotiation methods, fair labor practice studies, and mediation techniques. Pomeranz worked on Maxwell Street on weekends from the time he was fourteen years old through his college years. He was a puller in the early 1960s at a store called, Esquire Joe's, a clothing business at 714 West Maxwell. His job, as it was for all pullers, was to get customers into the store regardless of whether they wanted to shop there.

"I was trained by Harry Hartman, the brother-in-law of the store's owner," Pomeranz said. "My brother, Bill Pomeranz was a puller too."

Harry Hartman must have been quite a teacher. Jacob Pomeranz estimates he literally coaxed many hundreds of people into the store to buy. The job required a lot of psychology, a sense of humor and plenty of chutzpah. Pomeranz's explanation of his technique is classic.

"If you see a young man, you see he had a certain kind of swagger, you'd start to say, 'Oh, we've got great shirts.' and then you'd say, 'Ah, forget it, I can tell you don't have any money, so I'm not really interested in you.' And they'd say, 'Well, what do you mean?' And I'd say we've got great bargains but you still need to spend thirty bucks for a sweater, I can see you're not the kind of person that has thirty bucks. And they'd say, 'I sure do!' And you'd say, 'Naw come on, not your mother's milk money.' They'd say, 'I got the money!' So

JACOB POMERANCZ, 1966. Through high school and college Pomerancz, now a Chicago labor attorney, was a puller at a men's clothing store. He mastered the technique that talked and then pushed . . . or pulled . . . a reluctant shopper into the store. (Courtesy of Jacob Pomerancz.)

I'd say, 'Let's see the money.' They'd hand you thirty dollars and I'd say, 'OK. What color sweater do you want?' "

Pomeranz remembers there was a lot of touching involved, gentle grabbing as the puller sought to turn the passerby into a customer.

"There was a technique to the physical touching. You could move them from the sidewalk into the store physically. Virtually no one was offended that you were literally grabbing hold of them and shoving them into your store. You'd reach out and touch someone's elbow. If they're walking at right angles to you, you hold up your hand and your finger would hit their elbow and instinctively they would pivot and then with your other hand, you just put it on their shoulder and walk them into the store, chattering all the time about what great bargains you have.

"You could say the most insulting things, as long as you said it with a smile, as long as you kept the banter going. You could just about say anything to people.

"The thing that I learned on Maxwell Street," Pomeranz stressed, "is the main thing is the sale. If somebody is insulting you or not being nice to you, or being rude to you, you just sort of ignore all of that, you kept your eye focused on the main deal, which was making the sale."

Pomeranz remembers too that not only was making the sale imperative, so was keeping the sale. Where he worked, they had a shrewd, if not ethical way, of making sure no one returned merchandise.

"We weren't engaged in the business of building a brand there on Maxwell Street. We were not interested in customers returning. One way that was made clear was by the bags we'd put the garments in that we sold. They always bought bags that were seconds, like everything else that was for sale in the store. And so the bags had misprints of pizza parlors and so on, and that's what we'd put our garments in. So, if anybody came back with some kind of complaint, even thirty minutes later . . . of course we didn't give receipts out . . . we'd say, 'you didn't get that here.' And we'd say, 'let's see your bag.' And they'd show us the bag and we'd say, 'Does this look like a pizzeria?' "

Not a lot of pullers were women. But, Winnie Levine was a puller when she was twelve years old.

"My grandfather, Hyman Radousky, came to America from Kiev in Russia in the 1930s. He operated a store at 724 West Maxwell Street, Radousky and Son. At first he sold bicycles and bicycle parts. My grandfather would work in a dingy, dark basement. When he started he didn't have enough money to buy complete bicycles, so he took parts and assembled them, then sold them in the store."

As the years went by, Radousky and Son added furniture and toys to their stock and the business became somewhat of a variety store.

Ms. Levine lived with her grandparents. On Sundays, he didn't want her home alone as he, his wife, and other relatives worked in the store. So Winnie went to work as a puller.

"If you want a good deal," she remembers shouting as she stood next to a push cart, "go downstairs, ask for Ruby. Ask for Hyman. They'll give you a good price."

Winnie Levine spent her Sundays pulling people into her grandfather's store until she was sixteen years old.

"I would stand out there for long periods. I enjoyed being there. I learned how to deal with people, how to talk, how to ask for a discount. I learned bargaining."

*RUBY RADOUSKY IN THE **1960s.** He worked the inside of his father's variety store at 724 West Maxwell. His niece, Winnie Levine was one of the few women pullers. She started pulling when she was 12 years old. "If you want a good deal go downstairs, ask for Ruby." (Courtesy of Winnie Levine.)*

Another puller was Jack Rosenberg, whose father Max ran the Rose Tailor Shop on Maxwell Street. Jack, who wanted to be a cartoonist, was a puller at the Pazetsky clothing store before he started working in small night clubs as a comic and radio actor. In his act, he'd mimic the accents he learned from his father on Maxwell Street. Eighty-five-years-old when interviewed for this book, Jack could only remember one joke from his routine.

"I got married in a garage," Jack said. "And I couldn't back out."

Jack did remember how he pulled shoppers into Pazetsky's clothing store.

"People are walking down the street. A guy's coming near my store. I grab a hold of him and start talking. 'What are you looking for?' He says, 'Well, I want some pants.' I says, 'Jesus, I got all the god damn pants you want. Come on, come with me, I'll show you. 'Sam, take care of this gentleman, I know him for a long time, give him a break.' Once I got them into the store, the guys who were salesman, oh boy, a college education they didn't need, they could teach the college kids. 'Take care of this man here. I've known him for some time. Don't overcharge him, you understand?'

"Then, I'd go outside and get another mishuggene.* . . . Pullers were some of the best psychologists in the world," Jack said.

That was no joke.

*Mishuggene—(Misch–Schug–Ann–A) Yiddish. A screwball. A nutty person. Mostly used affectionately or without malice.

MAX ROSENBERG IN HIS MAXWELL STREET TAILOR SHOP. *His son Jack helped out in the shop and learned to mimic accents. Jack would use those accents in a night club comedy act. Jack was a puller before he started telling jokes for a living. "Pullers were some of the best psychologists in the world." (Courtesy of Jack Rosenberg.)*

JACK ROSENBERG, COMEDIAN AND ACTOR. *Jack Rosenberg played small clubs in Chicago when he was a comic and radio actor. He says he learned his comedic timing on Maxwell Street, working as a puller. (Courtesy of Jack Rosenberg.)*

JACK ROSENBERG, 2003. *At 85-years old, he could remember only one joke from his night club routine, but he never forgot his puller's technique. "Jesus, I got all the god-damn pants you want! Come on, come with me, I'll show you. Sam, take care of this gentleman." (Photo by Roger Schatz.)*

LERNER SHOE'S SALES TABLE. *In this 1937 photo, Israel Lerner, on the far left with the hat, joined employees and two of his sons at Lerner Shoe's sales table on the 800 block of west Maxwell Street. Irvin (Itzi) Lerner is fifth from the left, and Larry Lerner is second from the right. (Courtesy of the Chicago Historical Society.)*

There is a market for everything.

  Israel Lerner understood that. He bought old shoes that people left in shoe stores when they purchased a new pair.

  Mr. Lerner took those old shoes into the basement of the building where he lived with his wife and children at 1069 West Maxwell Street. Mr. Lerner put new soles on the shoes, shined them up and on Sundays, sold them on Maxwell Street.

  From such beginnings, around the end of World War I, Lerner Shoes came into being, and grew into one of the larger footwear businesses in the Maxwell Street area. Israel Lerner's son, Larry spent the first twenty years of his life in the shoe business. He helped his father, his mother, Jeannie, and his siblings grow the business.

  He was too young to remember those Saturday evenings when his father prepared the inventory in the basement for the Sunday market, but his mother always told him about what happened when it rained.

  "The basement where the shoes were kept would flood," Larry Lerner said. "The shoes

ISRAEL LERNER, HIS WIFE JEANNIE WITH CHILDREN LARRY AND SHIRLEY, 1927.
Larry learned the shoe business from his father on Maxwell Street. The family lived above the shoe store. During the Great Depression, to save money on coal in the winter, the Lerner's burned out-of-fashion shoes in a potbelly stove. (Courtesy of Larry Lerner.)

had to be reshined, and I remember my mother saying that sometimes when she picked up a shoe to clean it, a rat would jump out."

When Larry was about eight-years-old, the family moved the business to 815 West Maxwell, just a few doors off Halsted Street. They had a store on the second floor and the family lived on the third floor. Larry remembers his father paid about $13-a-month rent for both floors, and later, another $10 for a storage loft in a building next door.

"Every Sunday we'd take the shoes from the second floor downstairs onto the street and put them on a 50-foot-long table." (The insert photograph on the cover of this book was donated by the Lerner family to the Chicago Historical Society.) "In the wintertime, we had boots and if the customer wanted a pair of four-buckle boots, you had to try them on him. So, you had to sit him down, outside, and you had to wipe his shoes off in order to take the new boots and put the shoes on, you know, put the shoe into the boot. Sometime you couldn't get the shoe in, so you had to take a shmatte (rag) and put it around the damn shoes in order to slide the boot on, and these were things that my father not only did, my mother did it too.

"I remember my father buying shoes from a company on Roosevelt and Jefferson. We used to buy shoes and pay three-dollars and fifty cents per pair. We were very happy to sell it for three-dollars and seventy-five cents, to make a quarter. A quarter, at that time, could feed a family for dinner."

The Lerner's hard work kept them fed and the business growing.

"We were never hungry," Larry said. "Even though it was during the Depression, in the '30s, we were never hungry. My father was a good provider."

Larry spoke with great pride about his father's honesty. Israel Lerner resisted mobsters' demands that he sell stolen Florsheim Shoes. Luckily, the goons left him alone. Another son, Max, had run the store when the parents managed one of their very few vacations. While they were gone, Max Lerner bought a shipment of baby booties from someone who stopped in the store. Max paid five cents per pair and thought his father would be impressed. He was, but Larry remembers what his father taught all the sons that day.

"My father asked Max how much he paid for the baby shoes," Larry said.

" 'A nickel a pair,' Max answered." Larry said his father liked the price then asked for the bill.

" 'I have no bill,' Max said. My father told Max the shoes were stolen. We burned every pair in our potbelly stove."

Israel Lerner's business prospered. He expanded and became a shoe wholesaler also. Then the Depression came.

"We had thousands and thousand of pairs of women's pointed toe, lace-up shoes that they wore in the 1800s, with the hourglass heels. We couldn't afford to buy coal, and we would burn those shoes in the potbelly stoves. We couldn't sell them anyway because the style was so old."

Shoes that did sell included Converse gym shoes at 49 cents a pair.

After Pearl Harbor, Larry went to war. His father continued the business on Maxwell Street. When Larry returned from the service, he sold shoes for only a short time before joining his new wife Mildred's father in the liquor business.

"Maxwell Street enhanced my life," Larry Lerner said. "I remember shining shoes on Maxwell Street as a kid. I used to get a dime. When I got a dime, I retired."

He made more than a dime before retiring again. After leaving the liquor business, Larry and his brothers opened a shoe store on Milwaukee Avenue on Chicago's North Side.

"For 38 years I made a nice living there."

In the 1930s, Ed Siegel worked at a fruit stand owned by friends. He was always intrigued by how order emerged from all the chaos in the market area.

"All these people are milling about, thousands of people, screaming, yelling, music, singing, people selling snake medicine. But, there was order there. And the order was brought about by the market master, whose last name was Schuman. I don't know what his first name was. We called him Susie. And he would collect a dime a day from every single stand, if you had a stand that was two tables wide, you paid twenty cents."

Susie was really Sam Schuman. Shirley Derdiger, Susie's cousin, never knew his real name until he went into the army.

"He was the market manager," Ms. Derdiger said, "from the late '30s, through the '40s . . . took time out to go into the army . . . and went right back to his job through the '50s. He

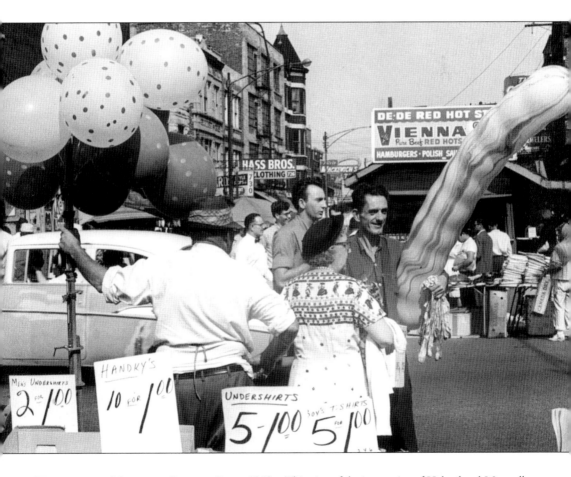

HALSTED AND MAXWELL STREET, LATE 1950S. *This view of the intersection of Halsted and Maxwell Street looks east. Market Masters kept order amidst the hundreds of street peddlers. (Courtesy of photographer Jack Davis.)*

was the most important person on Maxwell Street. Nobody could sell anything without his permission. He assigned the places where they could stand, where they could display their merchandise. He knew every storekeeper . . . they all knew him, I think that was more important, they all knew him, more so than who he knew. I can't tell you how Susie got the job. I know it was political, but it seems like it was something he had just for ever and ever. When I wanted something, I remember many years back, I wanted to buy a coat. So he said, 'Well, we're going out to Maxwell Street and see what I could do.' And, of course Susie took me into a very fine shop that from the outside didn't look like a fine shop. But, it was a wonderful shop and took me inside and said, 'This is my little cousin and you have to take very good care of her.' It was a very interesting thing because I knew what a very important person he was at that time."

Alan Lapping's grandfather, Harry Lapping, was the market master on Maxwell Street from 1918 through 1920. A good position, a responsible and powerful position . . . for a blind man.

"He'd go around with a seeing eye dog." Alan Lapping said. "He'd go to the stands, the carts, and collect in those days, two cents to a nickel for the right to spend the day on Maxwell Street."

"He knew everybody by the sound of their voice. He could tell who he was dealing with all the time. He was born and raised there and he was able to manage. He knew where they were located in this line, and had everything set up, so he knew the locations of one area from another, up and down the street."

"His job was to see that every person who had a cart paid a small fee. How much of that fee he kept, how much went to the city, I don't know but the worst it could be was a penny for him and a penny for the city because there wasn't much money involved."

The market master established one kind of order, and men like Patrick Angelo established another. Mr. Angelo became a Chicago police officer in 1955. His first assignment was in the Marquette District, which, at that time, included the Maxwell Street area. He patrolled on-foot and was well-known by most of the merchants.

"My job was to keep the peace and make sure all the shop owners knew I was there. I'd walk into the stores and let the owners know if they had any problems to just send for me or any other officer on the beat. I made detective in 1958 and was assigned to the police station at Maxwell and Morgan. I spent 36 years there."

Theft was a problem, and there always were unhappy shoppers calling police to complain about the deal they didn't get, but Angelo says the appearance of more violent crime came as the area began to change in the 1970s.

"There were some stabbings, shootings, and homicides, and we made several calls at the tavern and liquor store in Leavitt's Restaurant. If your tires were stolen the night before, you could go down to Maxwell Street and find them. This was in the later years."

Still, in the day-to-day cop's work, Mr. Angelo looks upon his years on Maxwell Street fondly. He always got a kick out of a vendor called "Socks," who hawked perfume.

"Socks sold his wares on the corner of Maxwell and Halsted. He'd get the perfume and throw it out onto the sidewalk to attract the people to his stand. Eventually, over the years, the perfume ate away the concrete, and you could see what the perfume did to the sidewalk."

Given his beat, Mr. Angelo may have inhaled the unforgettable aromas more than just about anyone on Maxwell Street.

"The people would go over to buy the hamburgers and hot dogs that you couldn't resist from the smell of the onions, and anyone who could walk by the stands selling the polish sausages and not buy one had to be sick."

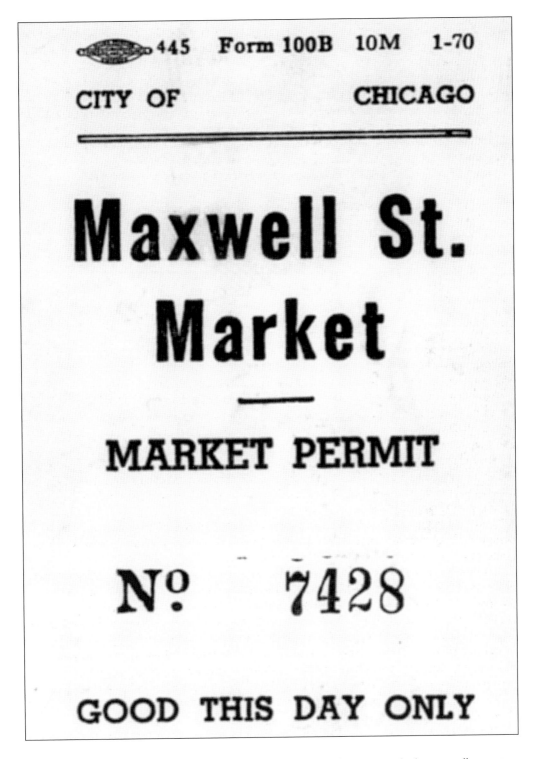

445 Form 100B 10M 1-70

CITY OF CHICAGO

Maxwell St. Market

—

MARKET PERMIT

N⁰ 7428

GOOD THIS DAY ONLY

MARKET PERMIT. *All street peddlers bought permits from the Market Master, who kept a small percentage. The balance went to the city. The earlier peddlers arrived, the better the location for their pushcarts and tables. (Courtesy of Nate Duncan.)*

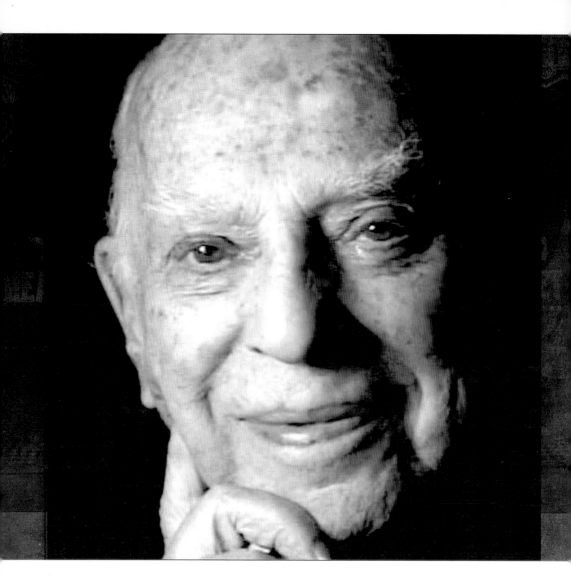

JUDGE ABRAHAM LINCOLN MAROVITZ. *Raised on Maxwell Street, he became the youngest state's attorney in Cook County, the first Jewish state senator in Illinois, a Superior Court Judge, Chief Judge of the Cook County Criminal Court, and in 1963, was nominated to the federal bench by President John F. Kennedy. Judge Marovitz was the last federal jurist not to have attended college. He served until his death in 2001 at age $95^1/_2$. A child of Lithuanian immigrants, it is believed he administered the oath of citizenship to more new Americans than any other jurist in U.S. history. His federal court rulings are among the fewest over-turned on appeals. (Videographed from the original in the Judge's federal court chambers.)*

4

The 95^1/$_2$ Year Old Mitzvah

Abraham Lincoln Marovitz

Note: The authors believe that on August 29, 1999, on his 94th birthday, Federal Judge Abraham Lincoln Marovitz, gave his last in-depth, videotaped interview. Judge Marovitz died March 17, 2001.

"A short, skinny, Jewish kid who hailed from Maxwell Street and never went to college became the biggest man in town."

–Andy Marovitz
at the memorial service for his grand-uncle, Abe.

It is absolutely accurate to say that Abraham Lincoln Marovitz was a Chicago icon. If there was a definite means to measure who was the most beloved public man in the city's history, he could win. In 20th-century Chicago he knew just about everybody in politics, sports, legal circles, and the entertainment business. He knew so many people, from all walks of life, that 1,700 came to his 90th birthday party in 1995. Thousands more would have been invited if they were alive. Abe Marovitz lived to be 95 years old. The late Mayor Richard J. Daley always said Abe Marovitz was his best friend. The Daley family, including Mayor Richard M. Daley always called him, "Uncle Abe."

"You didn't have to be important to be a friend of Abe Marovitz," the second Mayor Daley said when Abe died. "He took time out for all people regardless of who you were."

"He was a first-rate charmer," said attorney Richard J. O'Brien, who was once a Marovitz law clerk in the United States District Court in Chicago.

William L. Bauer, former Chief Judge of the Seventh U.S. Court of Appeals, was a close friend. "Abe Marovitz was one of the finest men any of us have known or will ever know."

Abraham Lincoln Marovitz led a life unlike anyone else.

He was a product of a wonderful mother and father, who lived, worked, and struggled to make a living in the Maxwell Street area. Having loving parents, absorbing the unique Maxwell Street education, and adhering to Jewish law and tradition were, of course, not exclusive to the Marovitz family. But, Abe's life possibly best exemplifies how strong values and virtues would prevail in the children of Maxwell Street despite the difficulties inherent to survival there.

Rachel Marovitz ran a small candy store and Joseph Marovitz was a tailor. Abe used to say his mother named him after Abraham Lincoln because she thought, having been shot in the temple by John Wilkes Booth, that Mr. Lincoln was Jewish.

Abe had two brothers and two sisters. They lived with their parents in three rooms behind the candy store. Abe was shaped by his life on Maxwell Street, but his mother's influence affected his soul.

"We learned from our ma and pa about just simple kindness," Judge Marovitz said in his federal court chambers. "We had to do what the Jews call a 'mitzvah,' a good deed. Every day my mom would kiss us and say, 'You gotta do your little mitzvah today,' and we'd come home and she'd ask us what we did for somebody else. And if we were fibbing, as we were every once-in-a-while, she could tell the moment we opened our mouths.

"Ma would say, 'Be a mench, be a man, be a good person. And everyday do your little mitzvah.' And at 94, I'm still doing them. It sounds kind of immodest, but the day is lost for me if I can't think of some little thing I did at the end of the day that made someone's lot just a little bit happier. You don't have to be a Phi Beta Kappa to do a mitzvah."

Mrs. Marovitz set an example many times.

"Kids would come into my mother's store and the candies were marked three for a penny or four for a penny. If five kids in a family came in, my ma would say, 'We got a sale today, five for a penny.'

"Now, ma used to sell stale milk for two cents cheaper or something. They'd come in to buy the stale milk and my mom would give them fresh milk and sell it for the sale price. She had dill pickles, where they'd stick a piece of lemon stick in there. She had a barrel with the pickles. You trusted the kids to put the penny in a cigar box she had. Instead of serving each kid, they helped themselves. And we learned to trust people.

"And mother would never tolerate anybody saying something un-nice about someone's other religion or color in that little candy store. And we saw how she handled people. My mom would say, 'My children don't hear that in here, and you can't talk like that, and just remember this: It takes the white and the black keys to play the Star Spangled Banner.' "

ABE MAROVITZ WITH HIS MOTHER, RACHEL, 1940s. He always said she was the kindest woman he ever knew. Her influence on him and his brothers and sisters was extraordinary. From her Maxwell Street home and candy store, she extolled her children to perform a mitzvah—a good deed— every day. (Courtesy of Chicago Historical Society.)

SWEARING IN. *As a Cook County Judge, Marovitz (left) swore in Chicago's new Mayor, Richard J. Daley in 1955 as Adlai Stevenson (left of Marovitz) and outgoing Mayor Martin Kennelly looked on. Judge Marovitz swore Daley into office after every one of Daley's election victories. (Videographed from the original in the Judge's federal court chambers.)*

LIKE FATHER, LIKE SON. *Judge Marovitz administers the oath of office to Mayor Richard M. Daley as the Mayor's wife, Maggie and children look on. All the Daley's called the Judge, "Uncle Abe." (Videographed from the original in the Judge's federal court chambers.)*

Born in 1905, Abraham Lincoln Marovitz rose from his humble Maxwell Street beginnings to become the youngest assistant state's attorney in Cook County history, a lawyer in private practice, a state senator, a Sergeant Major in the United States Marines, a Superior Court Judge, and then Chief Judge of the Cook County Criminal Courts. In 1963, President John F. Kennedy appointed him to the federal bench where he served until his death in 2001.

Legions of lawyers would testify that Abe Marovitz was a great jurist. He was fair, just, and would often say his success had much to do with advice his mother gave him back on Maxwell Street.

"Mother would always say, if we got into a little argument, 'Children, you've got to learn how to disagree without being disagreeable,' and that stayed with me all my life. I settled more cases, they tell me, than most judges over here. Bringing people together. And the technique I learned from my ma and pa."

He certainly didn't learn it in college.

Abe Marovitz never went to college. He was the last federal judge in the nation without a college degree. He graduated from Medill High School, just a few blocks from Maxwell Street. When he wasn't trying to make a few dollars boxing, Abe was an office boy at the prestigious law firm of Meyer, Rothstein, and Platt.

After one particularly tough boxing match, 16 year-old Abe returned to the office where Mr. Rothstein asked about the cuts and bruises on his face.

"He said, 'You can't be much of a boxer. Is that what you want to be? How far did you go in school?' I said I just finished high school. He said, 'Go over to Kent, it's a night law

SERGEANT MAJOR ABRAHAM LINCOLN MAROVITZ. *Wounded by Japanese shrapnel, he refused his Purple Heart, saying too many "leathernecks" were more seriously hurt. The corpsman who treated his wounds became a Chicago alderman. Marovitz had to sentence him to prison. (Videographed from the original in the Judge's federal court chambers.)*

RECEIVING THE DECALOGUE SOCIETY HONOR. *Jake Arvey, possibly the most powerful Jewish politician in Chicago history, and himself a product of Maxwell Street, joins Mayor Richard J. Daley in congratulating Abraham Lincoln Marovitz as he received a Decalogue Society honor. Arvey met Marovitz when the Judge was an assistant state's attorney, and gave him an influential position in the mostly Jewish 24th Ward on Chicago's West Side. (Videographed from the original in the Judge's federal court chambers.)*

school.' I said, I don't have any money. You're only paying me ten bucks a week. So he says, 'Go over there and register.' And he paid my tuition, my initiation fee, and my dues. When I got out of there I was only 19 years old. It was 1924. Had to be 21 to take the Bar. Had to wait two years to take the Bar, and all the time I worked for him as his office boy. When I passed the Bar, he didn't know what to do with me so he put me in the state's attorney's office."

Abe Marovitz spent six years with the state's attorney. It was there that he came to the attention of 24th Ward boss, Jake Arvey, the powerful Jewish Democrat who later became chairman of the Cook County Democratic Party.

By 1939, Marovitz was in the Illinois Senate, the first Jew to serve there. That's when his friendship with Richard J. Daley grew close.

Throughout the early years of his career, Abe was performing the mitzvahs his mother had urged on him back in earlier days on Maxwell Street. Those acts of kindness would become legendary. There was even a mitzvah of sorts he performed for his country.

In 1943, at the age of 38, and comfortably in the Illinois Senate, Abe Marovitz tried to enlist in the United States Marine Corps. Because of his age, and his colorblindness, he was going to be rejected. But he used some of the political clout he'd accumulated and got into uniform. When the Marines wouldn't send him overseas, he called a fellow Illinois Democrat who was an assistant secretary of the Navy, and demanded to be shipped into a Pacific combat area. Reluctantly, Adlai Stevenson pulled some strings and Abe went to war.

Rising to the rank of sergeant major, Abe was wounded by shrapnel in the Philippines. He refused his Purple Heart, saying too many other men were more seriously wounded.

Abe never married, although he did have an almost life-long relationship with a woman who wasn't Jewish. Friends said both had promised their families they would not marry outside their religions. Yet, it isn't so much of an exaggeration to say that Abe had one of the biggest families anywhere. He treated everyone he met as if they were relatives. To him, it was a mitzvah to do so.

"My ma used to say, 'There's an art to making friends, children, but there's a greater art in keeping them.' "

The judge honored his parents by living the life they taught him to live, and in all the speeches he gave over the years . . . and sometimes he'd give several a day...he remembered them always. He also remembered them in another extraordinary way. Abe always wore a pair of cufflinks designed with images of his parents. He was never without those cufflinks. They were always in his pocket when he didn't wear a cufflinked shirt.

"My pa was the most honest man I knew, and my ma the kindest person I've ever known."

After his death, at the memorial service held in the Federal Court building in Chicago, Judge Marovitz's Maxwell Street heritage, and the love he had for his mother and father were mentioned often. Those who eulogized him spoke of his mitzvahs. Monsignor Ignatius D. McDermott said, "Daily, Abe's game plan was to perform his mitzvahs by stealth and to have them discovered by accident. He wrote every noble deed on ice cubes."

The mitzvahs continued even after Abe died. Several charities received millions of dollars in donations from the Judge Marovitz trust, and another million dollars went to the Chicago Bar Foundation for scholarship programs. The judge's priceless collection of Abraham Lincoln items, books, pamphlets, prints, busts, letters, and photographs, were donated to the Abraham Lincoln Presidential Library and Museum in Springfield, Illinois.

As he spoke of his mother, during the interview for the documentary about Maxwell Street, Judge Marovitz recited his mother's favorite poem:

> *There is kindness, human kindness that the world needs most today.*
> *Not so much talk of duty, but a friendly kindly way.*
>
> *Sometimes the good are selfish, and the righteous stern and cold.*
> *But the kind are always welcome, because kindness never grows old.*
>
> *And there is no force more potent, than a gracious act or smile.*
> *'Tis the kindly men and women, that make our lives worthwhile.*

Abe Marovitz always said he was not a self-made man. He said others aided him throughout his life. His friends might argue the point, but one of them, Judge William J. Bauer may have captured exactly what it was that made Abe tick.

"He took the best of everything he heard, the best from everybody he knew, his mother, his father, his mentors, his brothers, his dear friends . . . took their best and put it into action."

Note: The extensive Marovitz photograph collection is now part of the judge's papers in the Richard J. Daley Library at the University of Illinois at Chicago.

JOEY'S TAB

Joey Harris was one of the 1,700 people invited to Abe Marovitz's 90th birthday party in 1995. The judge pointed him out to the crowd to say that Harris was the first person he knew with a charge account. Their mothers were friends and Mrs. Harris would run a tab at Rachel Marovitz's candy store, mostly for candy and after school snacks for her son. Then, she'd pay once a week.

Mr. Harris smiled as he told the story.

"Abe told the crowd that I was the first guy that he knew with a charge account. Abe remembered how my mother used to send me to school and after school, I was seven, eight years old, I'd go into his mother's store and get milk, halavah,* and my mother would come in to pay on Friday before Shabbas. Eighteen cents, twenty cents."

Joey Harris grew up in the Maxwell Street area, near Jefferson Street, a few blocks east of Halsted. His father, a leather cutter for the Lytton Store on State Street, worked weekends on Maxwell Street to earn some extra money.

An immigrant from Russia, Joey's father came up with an idea to sell a truly Russian beverage.

"He decided to sell Kvass. Kvass is like a Coca-Cola, it's a Russian drink made from bread. So he got me up at two o'clock on Wednesday morning, just him and I, and I was seven, eight years old, he'd take me in the basement and we'd manufacturer kvass. This was during Prohibition and this was a drink that was almost alcoholic. And he'd bring it down on Maxwell Street, we'd get up early in the morning and he'd put ice in the wagon, he'd put the kvass in bottles, and in an hour we were sold out, we were out of business. I used to ask my father, why don't you make more, but he didn't want to make more than three or four dollars. He said he was happy because he worked four hours instead of working all day Sunday."

*Halavah—hall-VAH or HALL-vah—A Turkish or East Indian candy made with honey, and usually ground sesame seeds and farina. There are fruit and nut varieties.

ONCE A MAXWELL STREET MARINE, ALWAYS A MAXWELL STREET MARINE. *Abraham Lincoln Marovitz is honored at his 90th birthday party in 1995. Joey Harris and 1,700 guests came to offer their best wishes to the man who left the Illinois Senate at the age of 38 to join the Marine Corps in 1943. Marovitz was colorblind and had to pull strings to enlist. He pestered Adlai Stevenson to get him assigned overseas. (Videographed from the original in the Judge's federal court chambers.)*

Both of attorney Herb Kanter's grandfathers had businesses in the Maxwell Street area. One ran a grocery store in the basement of a building at 13th and Newberry. The other was a blacksmith.

"Abraham Lincoln Marovitz's family was close with my mother's family. His father was a tailor and my grandfather was a blacksmith. In preparation for Passover, the Marovitz's would burn their chomets* in my grandfather's blacksmith shop. Abe was one of my sponsors when I was inducted to practice before the United States Supreme Court."

One of Kanter's prized possessions is the very rare Yiddish and English text of the U.S. Constitution, which his grandfather Phillip Kanter, the grocer, studied while preparing for his citizenship test.

Like his grandfathers, Herb Kanter worked on Maxwell Street.
In fact, he worked there with Ira Berkow, author of *Maxwell Street: Survival in a Bazaar*, (Garden City: Doubleday & Co.1977).

"I went to grammar school with Ira Berkow," Kanter said. "We used a radio flyer wagon to bring our goods to our stand on the street. We sold women's nylons and men's cotton socks. I was selling nylons, three pair for a dollar, had to be careful to conceal the holes in the nylons or men's stockings."

Chomets—Yiddish term for food that is leavened and not kosher for Passover.

HERB KANTER, 1950s. Both his grandfathers had businesses in the Maxwell Street area. He remembers chasing his clothing inventory when it blew off his stand during a major thunderstorm. (Courtesy of Herb Kanter.)

די קאָנסטיטוציע
פון די פאַראייניגטע שטאַטען.
ענגליש און יידיש.

איבערגעזעצט פון
אלכסנדר האַרקאַווי.

מיט ביילאַגע:
דער סיטיזען.

The Constitution of the United States.

ENGLISH AND YIDDISH.

Translated by
ALEXANDER HARKAVY.

To which is added:

The CITIZEN.

A GUIDE TO NATURALIZATION
REVISED EDITION

Copyright, 1922, by the Hebrew Publishing Co., New York
1932
Printed in the U.S.A.

PHILLIP KANTER'S *1932* YIDDISH/ENGLISH VERSION OF THE CONSTITUTION OF THE UNITED STATES. *Mr. Kanter studied the translations to prepare for his citizenship test. (Courtesy of Herb Kanter.)*

Phillip and Anna Kanter, Herb Kanter's Grandparents. 1913. *Martin Kanter, Herb's father is seated, left. Seymour, an uncle is on Phillip Kanter's lap. (Courtesy of Herb Kanter.)*

When Berkow viewed the documentary from which this book derives, he noted his days on the street.

"From 1951–1956 I sold stockings on the corner at Maxwell and Halsted. I was in several locations starting at 719 Maxwell," Berkow wrote. "I owned a belt stand from 1956–1959 at Jefferson and Maxwell."

While Berkow sold belts, Herb Kanter moved on to other jobs in the area.

"My last job on Maxwell Street was for 'Smilin' Lou, The Angel of Maxwell Street. I sold men's work clothes there at Maxwell and Newberry. Every weekend when I'd go down to the store, we'd get ten dollars if we had to work or not. So every morning I'd tell Lou that really, it looks like rain today, although the sun could be out nice and bright. This one morning, in the late '50s, it was overcast and really looked like trouble, I said 'Lou, I don't think we should open up this morning,' but we opened up our stand, long card tables plus racks of clothing. And then the skies opened up. There was a seich that day on Lake Michigan. I guess some people fishing along the pier in Chicago drowned and it was a terrible storm, and we were chasing shirts down the street. We lost a lot of merchandise. And it was cold in the winter. We'd be at our stand, we'd bundle up and the customers came. It was just as crowded in the winter as it was in the summer."

5.

Gun Runner with a Heart
GIVE AND GIVE, AND GIVE AGAIN

"Forget about business! We've got to see that the Haganah has the arms and everything!"

–Joseph Robinson

Weapons were not in the usual inventory of Robinson's Department Store on Maxwell Street. One of the most successful businesses over the street's long history, Robinson's, at 657 West Maxwell, was famous for selling the best Mah-Jongg sets, chandeliers, and oriental rugs. Robinson's was the only store that always advertised its guarantees and promised money back to any unsatisfied customers. Joseph Robinson could explain exactly how the Chinese and Persian rug makers could line up the dyes so perfectly that the colors would never bleed into one another, and last for generations. He was a salesman's salesman.

Joseph Robinson was also a very religious, Jewish man. His was the only one of the large department stores that always closed on the Sabbath and all Jewish holidays. Then in 1948, with the founding of the new State of Israel, Robinson became a gun-runner. His sons Sheldon and Jerome proudly tell the stories of that episode in their father's life.

"One time there was a place called the Lawndale Pool Room. And you walk into the Lawndale Pool Room, all you'd see is card-playing there, and you saw the people there. First of all, you'd be afraid to walk in there," said Jerome Robinson.

"They had guns with shoulder holsters. I mean these were all Mafia people. The Jewish Mafia," offered Sheldon Robinson.

"If a Jew was getting hurt or got hurt by some Polish people who came around from other areas, that place emptied out, with all the money on the table. Emptied out. They went out to see what they can get, or whoever they can get. Not only that, I remember my father, in the time of the 1948 War in Israel, they needed guns, they needed Jeeps, they needed everything. He went out to people like those in the Lawndale Pool Room and he told them, 'Stop, gentlemen,' I mean you took your life in your hands when you went into this place, 'Stop gentlemen, stop all this card-playing. I need money for the Haganah.'* Money just came. Flowed into the man," said Jerome Robinson.

"The store was irrelevant," said Sheldon Robinson. "He says, 'Forget about business! We've got to see that the Haganah has the arms and everything!' Well, he went around and bought guns. He went around and—all illegal—you weren't allowed to do any of this. And he had all kinds of stuff shipped into our store. We then packed it with clothing that we had. It was sent to the Army or to whoever needed it in Israel. And packed it in packages. But how do you get it from the United States to Israel, when you know it's illegal transporting of arms? There was

* *Haganah-* Hebrew word for defense. The name of Israel's pre-independence army.

JOSEPH ROBINSON. He brought scores of Holocaust survivors to America and gave them merchandise to go into business on Maxwell Street. Robinson responded to Jewish causes by often putting himself and his business in jeopardy. He ran guns and supplies through his store and arranged shipping to Israel during the 1948 War of Independence. (Courtesy Eshel Productions.)

a fast freight company owned by a Jewish firm. And we used to have lots of stuff coming in through this freight company. So my father called up. He says, 'Look, I'm supplying this.' He says, 'I'm supplying the label to package it.' He says, '*I'm* taking the chance. *You've* got to see to it that the transportation goes to New York, and from New York, gets on the ship. We will have people in New York.'

"Well, that's how arms got in. And on the bill of lading it said 'Clothing for the poor.' The bill of lading said all kinds of lies. The chances that he took were… this was federal… this was very, very dangerous. But, at that time, that's what he did in order to help Israel. And he raised thousands and thousands of dollars. Like my brother was telling you, he raised loads and loads of money."

In 1899, Yossel Robinson was born in Russia. Translated from the Yiddish, Yossel was Joseph, and after coming to the United States at age seven, Yossel became Joseph. He first lived in Chicago with his parents and four brothers on O'Brien Street, just one block north of Maxwell Street. One of the brothers, William, was a lawyer, a long-time president of the Jewish United Fund and influential in Chicago's Democratic politics, which included close ties with Jacob Arvey. Arvey was one of the most powerful men in Illinois politics and another product of Maxwell Street. Both Bill Robinson and Jake Arvey proved influential when Joseph Robinson's acts of charity and good intentions needed a little old fashioned clout.

"My father did amazing things for the Jewish people," Sheldon Robinson said admiringly. "One case, for example, it was during the Prohibition days. You couldn't buy whiskey and you're not allowed to sell whiskey. Unless you were Al Capone. There was an old Jewish guy with a beard. He had fourteen children. And he would go all the time with a buggy, and there was a baby in the buggy, cause he always had, with fourteen children, he always had a baby. Under the baby there was hooch. You know, he had whiskey or whatever he was selling. And the federal authorities knew this man, and they had picked him up and put him into jail many times. They finally put him into the federal penitentiary. Here's a man with fourteen kids to support, right? The community got together, and I remember my father got together money, and bought the guy a store so he could own a butcher shop. But, it didn't help. He made hooch in the back of the store and got caught again. My father got my Uncle Bill and Jack Arvey involved to try and help the guy. They went to President Roosevelt himself, who pardoned him."

Joseph Robinson was raised with an understanding that you helped those in need. Often someone without a job was hired in the department store, whether there was a need for more workers or not. While there are many such stories coming from Maxwell Street, the Robinson family, Joseph Robinson most particularly, were always giving.

If wealth was measured only by money, then Robinson was never truly a wealthy man. He came to Maxwell Street a child of a poor immigrant family. He eventually bought the business he worked in which became the Robinson's Department Store. But during the Depression, Robinson went bankrupt. But, eventually he paid off every cent he owed. In the Depression years, such devotion to one's financial responsibilities and the ability to meet them entirely was rare, not only on Maxwell Street, but everywhere.

Joseph Robinson surely learned from his mother.

Becky Robinson worked tirelessly for Jewish organizations.

"My grandmother," Sheldon recalls, "would go out to everybody, to all of Uncle Bill's friends. She'd go up to these people and sell them tickets for a fish dinner to raise money for the Hebrew Parochial School. And I remember she went up to one multi-millionaire and asked him for money. He said to her, 'Mrs. Robinson, you didn't have to come here. You could have called me on the phone. I would have sent you a check.' My grandmother says, 'Well, I wanted to see you personally to make sure I get the money.' The millionaire gave her a check and then says, 'Look, my chauffeur is downstairs. He will take you home. Don't take a bus, don't get on a streetcar.' So my grandmother went with the chauffeur, but he didn't return until eight or nine o'clock that night. She had the chauffeur take her all over the city to raise money."

That story is remembered fondly by the Robinson family, but another need to raise money—after World War II began in Europe—is one of the truly extraordinary moments in Maxwell Street history. Of course, Joseph Robinson was at the center of it all.

"A rabbi, Rabbi Herschberg," Jerome Robinson remembers, "was in France during the war. Hitler needed cash and the rabbi heard that the Nazis would free 500 Jews over the French border for five-thousand dollars. Either the Jews would be freed or slaughtered. I'll never forget it. A long-distance call came into the store from France. Now who made such calls? The war was on. It took hours to place a call, and here, we were getting a call. I answered the phone. 'Who is it?' He says, 'It's Rabbi Herschberg.' I says, 'Rabbi Herschberg, where are you?'

JOSEPH ROBINSON, C. 1940. Pictured in the center, Joseph Robinson is seen here with some of the employees inside Robinson's Department Store. The merchandise in the store was often of the highest quality. Oriental rugs, chandeliers, and Mah-Jongg sets were good sellers. (Courtesy of Sheldon Robinson.)

He says, and I knew him, he says, 'I'm in France now. I must talk with Reb** Yossel.' I says, 'Just a second, I'll get my father on the phone.' He says, 'I need five-thousand dollars wired by tomorrow morning. He says, 'We can get five hundred Jews across the border immediately if you immediately get me five thousand dollars.' "

Joseph Robinson got on the line and talked with the impatient rabbi. "I'll do what I can," Jerome recalls his father saying.

"My father went out to the banks and starts to borrow money, from the banks, starts to sign notes all over. He still couldn't get it all. But he got other people, business people. I remember he went to Glavin Brothers, a big, big furniture place. He went to people, big business and told 'em, 'Here's what's happening.' He says, 'Trust me with this. I'm not stealing money.' Now everybody knew Joe Robinson was honest. He said he was taking the money, it's not for himself, he's not pocketing it and running. But he raised the money and wired the money. Now, I didn't even know how to wire money. He went to the bank, and the bank said they'd handle the wire for him. They wired the money and the people crossed the border."

After the war it was Joseph Robinson once again taking a lead in helping victims of the Nazis. He sponsored scores of Holocaust survivors as they came into the United States, and then to Chicago and Maxwell Street.

"My father, first of all, he owned a store," Sheldon related. "We owned two apartment buildings, small apartment buildings and the United States said that you could bring over people from Europe, refugees, only if you could get them a visa, if you can give them a job and if you can give them a place to live. Well, we signed affidavits in blank. I remember we copied our tax reports, we made them in sets, and I'm telling you hundreds and hundreds of sets of these were sent over through the Hebrew Immigrant Aid Society."

"My father always said, 'You just give to Jewish people. Save lives, all right?' "

"And those people started to come in," Sheldon went on. "They had to come to Chicago because that's what the visa required. They had nothing. They didn't ask for money, but they wanted to make a living somehow. So what we'd do is that my father would just take merchandise off the shelves, give it to them and say, 'Here's a board and two horse supports to hold the board. Go out on Maxwell Street on Sunday and peddle. You'll make money.' And that's what they did. And many of these people became very wealthy in later years. But they needed a start, and that's how my father helped."

Hundreds of such people were selling on Maxwell Street.

"Today I see some of them," says Sheldon, "older people who say, 'When I first came to America, Yossel Robinson gave me some merchandise. I'd go down to the street and I sold. I made some sales and that was enough for me to eat for that day.' These were all the people that came over with the tattoos on their arms, with their numbers."

Joseph Robinson never asked for paybacks. Never. Because he so often performed anonymous acts of good will, there are many people who never knew it was he who provided a Sabbath meal, or arranged a job for them. Those who knew of his generosity and humanity, who tried to return his favors, were politely told no.

Joseph Robinson died in the 1970s. His sons were once asked whether God would be good to their father. Sheldon Robinson answered with his father's own words.

"I'll get paid back. I'll get paid back where I'm supposed to get paid back."

Reb—Yiddish—Used to address a highly respected religious man.

SURVIVING AGAIN

Note: Paul Federman died in November, 2003, at the age of 82. When interviewed he was not well. It was very difficult for him to speak. Federman's son, Irving tells his father's Maxwell Street story. The only sentence Paul Federman could relate clearly, describes how he first encountered Hitler's troops in World War II.

It was 1939. German troops were starting their march through Poland and killing Jews. At a synagogue in a small village, Paul Federman and two brothers, fleeing the Nazis, were given a horse and wagon. They slept in the wagon, then decided to try and return to where

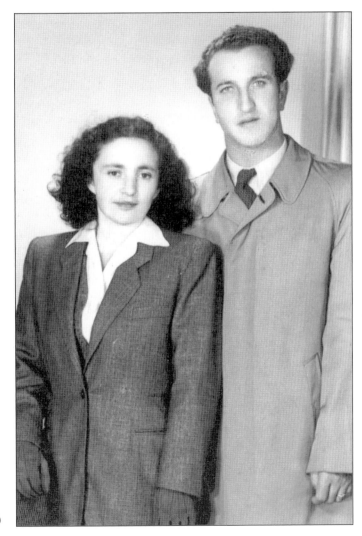

PAUL FEDERMAN AND HIS WIFE, GIZI. They met in a displaced persons camp in Germany after surviving the Holocaust. He arrived on Maxwell Street with virtually nothing and eventually owned four clothing businesses. (Courtesy of Irving Federman.)

Paul and Gizi Federman with Sons, Irving, on the left, and Alan. *All worked in Paul's clothing businesses on Maxwell and Halsted Streets. Paul Federman first worked as a butcher at Goldblatt's on 47th and Ashland and spent weekends selling off a push-cart on Maxwell Street. (Courtesy of Irving Federman.)*

their mother and father were living. They took the wagon and quickly were engulfed by advancing Germans. A moment that could have been the end of their lives miraculously was the beginning of a six-year survival of the Holocaust.

Paul Federman never forgot.

"About six o'clock we meet the whole German army. They stopped us. They unhitched the wagon. They wanted the horse. They told us to stay overnight at a farm along the highway."

Irving Federman tells the rest of the story.

"My father, being a young man of twenty, hid in the field of a farmer with his two brothers for three or four years. They were able to pay the farmer to keep them, and the farmer, at the risk of losing his own life, did that, and my father and his brothers survived the Holocaust.

"My father's family and my mother's family were both victims of the Holocaust. My father's family in Poland was very large. Actually, there were about nine or ten brothers and sisters."

Paul and his two brothers were the only Federman's the Nazis didn't kill. They were in a displaced persons camp in Germany after the war. That's where he met his wife, who along with two of her sisters had survived the Auschwitz concentration camp and a slave labor camp.

Paul married in Germany and immigrated to the United States, having survived the post-war time in Germany buying and selling on the black market.

After about a year in Pennsylvania, Paul and his wife came to Chicago.

"My father spoke Polish and Yiddish, and went to school to learn English at the JPI (Jewish People's Institute) . . . on Roosevelt Road," said Irving. "He worked as a butcher at Goldblatt's at 47th and Ashland, a Polish neighborhood, because he was able to communicate fluently in Polish."

Paul Federman spent weekends selling clothing off a wooden board on Maxwell Street.

"He didn't have a car," Irving said. "He would keep his things in a box in a home owned by gypsies on Maxwell Street. He would pay them to keep the goods there, then he'd get the goods from them on Sunday and go out to the stand and sell the stuff on the stand. My brother Alan and I would come down with my mother. I must have been five or six years old. We'd take the bus. At that time, we were living in Albany Park, which is a long bus ride, about an hour or so, several buses to get down to meet him at the stand."

Running the stand was a family affair.

"It was our job to stand there and watch for the gonifs, you know, the thieves."

In 1959, Goldblatt's closed the butcher shop, and Paul decided to work full-time on Maxwell Street. With a little help from relatives, he opened his first store at 704 West Maxwell and called it Paul's Bargain Store.

"My father would rarely let any customer walk out of the store without selling him something, even if he had to make very, very little profit. And the customers that would come there regularly, at some point knew this, that they could get a very low price from him, because he always wanted to sell something. He'd like to make a good profit, but if he couldn't make a good profit, he'd take less of a profit, and if he could only make a little profit, he'd take that, because he'd rather exchange the item, get the money, and have the customer come back. But customers knew that if they bargained with him long enough, they were going to get a better price than they could get anywhere else."

Paul Federman had to sell a lot of clothing to make a living that way. He did, and he worked everyday except for the Jewish High Holidays. There was the one store from 1959 and then in 1970, when Irving was nineteen and brother, Alan, twenty-one, their father

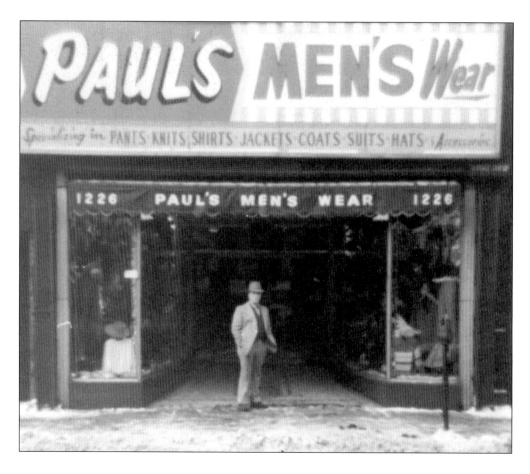

PAUL FEDERMAN IN FRONT OF ONE OF HIS STORES ON HALSTED STREET. *(Courtesy of Irving Federman.)*

opened a second store, this one at 1226 South Halsted. That store was Paul's Men's Wear. Irving and Alan, both in college, ran the new store.

"In the early '70s, business was booming," Irving remembers. "Actually, it wasn't that difficult, and we did a good job, and we were easier for customers to get along with than my father was. We were very successful with two stores, and I was going to the University of Illinois at Chicago, and I went to law school in 1973 to 1976 at Loyola University. And, I was also working at the store."

A third store came next.

"In 1973, my father rented the place next door, 1212 South Halsted. It had been a furniture store before. And at that time, we had three places. By 1975 or 1976, my father eventually closed the store altogether on Maxwell Street because it was just too much to try to be in all the stores at the same time. And, the 1212 store was becoming successful. Actually, he was very moved and sad, very emotional when he had to close the store on Maxwell Street because it had been such a big part of his life, where he got his start."

Paul Federman, however, wasn't finished expanding his business. In 1979, forty years after Nazi soldiers took his horse but not him, he became owner of what many always

ALAN AND IRVING FEDERMAN IN THE 1970S. *They helped their father in his stores. Irving became an attorney. Alan operates Adam Joseph, a clothing store on Roosevelt Road. (Courtesy of Irving Federman.)*

believed was the premier location in the market.

"1200 South Halsted became available," said Irving. "This location was once the home of Turner Brothers, a premier clothing store in Chicago founded in 1901. Turner retired and closed the store. He sold the building to my father. I was a Cook County state's attorney at the time, and my father asked that I open up the new store and run the store. I did and I began my own law practice in a little office upstairs. I had some managers that helped me run the store."

The store at 1200 South Halsted, on the southwest corner of the Roosevelt Road intersection, was one of the last to close as the University of Illinois moved to demolish and develop the area. Alan Federman operates a smaller clothing business on Roosevelt Road near Clinton today.

"My father's experience is probably very representative of what Maxwell Street represents," Irving said. "You have somebody who survived what he survived in the Holocaust, losing everything, coming to this country with virtually nothing, being unable to speak the language, and there was a place called Maxwell Street. There he could come and make a living and make money, and he could start at the very bottom, using a stand, then a store and really, winding up in the flagship of all the stores in the area. This is what he lived to do. That's maybe what he survived for."

PAUL FEDERMAN'S FIRST STORE WAS AT 704 WEST MAXWELL STREET. *He called it Paul's Bargain Store. In 1979, 40 years after a brush with Nazi troops in Poland, he bought one of the best locations in the Maxwell Street market—the former Turner Brothers Clothing Store at 1200 South Halsted. (Courtesy of Irving Federman.)*

LOVE YOUR COMPETITION

Throughout most of his youth, Sherwin Cherry worked in his father's business, Jack's Shoe Store, at 728 West Maxwell Street. Sherwin was on the job there almost every Saturday and Sunday.

JACOB "JACK" CHERRY. 1930s. *He gave loans to competitors and never charged any interest. He operated his shoe store on Maxwell Street for more than 30 years. (Courtesy of Sherwin Cherry.)*

"The store was in the basement. Everybody knew my father. His real name was Jacob, he went by Jack. In fact, on the street he was called, Yonney. I don't know why. He had a partner, his name was Irving Linn, but he was better known as Jesus. His nickname was Jesus. I don't know why either. They had the store for 30 years till they both retired when Maxwell Street was losing its luster in the late 1960s.

"My father and Irving bought the store from my uncle, Jake Savitt. He let them pay it out over time. This was 1932."

Sherwin Cherry has always been fascinated by the way his father and other merchants would help each other, even if they were in direct competition.

"They called the guy who owned the shoe store across the street, 'The Greener.' I don't know why. My father and Irving would trade shoes with him if he had a customer and needed a size. There was such camaraderie of all the Jewish people, how they stuck together. Even though they were competitors. I can remember my father loaning money to a couple other shoe merchants on the street. One wanted to go into business and one just because he bought so much merchandise that they would loan him money, and it could be a couple thousand dollars. Come Sunday night, this merchant would come back and pay him back. There was never no signing, no nothing. There was never any interest.
My father got nothing out of it. We don't see that today."

6.

Pants Maybe, But Definitely We'll Eat
LYON'S DELICATESSEN/NATE'S DELI

Maxwell Street smelled.

The aromas could attack your senses. After all, most of the food items were available on open wagons, or hot dog stands built from scrap wood that could be removed at the end of the day. Ice was the preferred, sometimes the only refrigeration in the earlier days. Butcher shops emitted odors. Fish carts attracted and repelled at the same time. Chickens, ducks, and geese were penned or tied up awaiting their ritual kosher slaughter. And the grilled onions that were slapped on hot dogs left the kind of marvelous aroma that remains with you the rest of your life.

Inside Lyon's Delicatessen and Grocery, just west of Halsted Street at 807 West Maxwell, the smell of fine kosher foods drew huge numbers of hungry shoppers on a weekend. There were never more than three tables in the place. Most of the trade came in for carry-out or called Haymarket 1-9396 to place an order.

Corned beef sandwiches on rye bread were the big seller. In the winter, Lyon's sold more than a thousand cups of coffee on Sundays. Lyon's customers also came for pastrami, rolled beef, smoked goose breast, and other meats soaked with cholesterol-heavy fats that today just aren't used anymore. Lox and smoked chub were but some of the many fish items always available. And the pickled herring was legendary.

The recipe for that pickled herring belonged to Sara Lyon. Like her husband, Abraham, Sara came to the United States from Latvia just about the time of the World's Fair . . . the Columbia Exposition . . . which opened in Chicago in 1893.

Ben Lyon, who will be 96 years old at publication of this story, in relatively good health, and living alone in Skokie, reminisced about his parents.

"They didn't know each other at the time. My mother went to work for a blouse factory, making women's blouses. My father was a cigar maker. Eventually they met, they got together and they married, and my father and my mother opened up a little grocery store on 14th Place, near Halsted in Chicago."

That was how the family business started. It is also where the family started. Ben was born there in 1908. Two sisters, one older, one younger, were born there also.

"Eventually, the place was too small . . . we lived in the back of the store . . . and found another place at 1302 South Jefferson. We also lived in the back of the store but there was a little more room there."

Ben Lyon remembers the telephone number of the Jefferson store, Canal 6-7258.

"My earliest memory was on Jefferson Street before we moved on Maxwell Street. I was, perhaps, seven or eight years old. I use to stand up on a little stool, so I could wait on the customers."

LYON'S DELICATESSEN IN THE 1930S. *Ben Lyon's father and mother started the business on Jefferson Street and moved to 807 West Maxwell in 1924. The deli was always a central gathering place for merchants and shoppers. (Courtesy of Ben Lyon.)*

The business moved to the Maxwell Street location in 1924. Ben was 16 years old. He would remain in the store until retiring in 1973. In 1933, Ben married the landlord's daughter.

"I got married in 1933 to a lovely woman. In fact, her mother was our landlord in the building . . . not that I got a break in the rent over there.

"Her name was Cele Lyon. And in later years, she used to come down and help me on the weekends, just on weekends. But she never worked full-time in the store. Her mother was fairly rich, and her mother never wanted her to go out with me. She was looking for a rich young man to marry her daughter. But after we got married, I became one of her favorites, so everything worked out.

"I got married during the height of the Depression. And, I went right to work. I was making twenty-five dollars a week at the time, which was a lot of money, 'cause everything else was so cheap. Everything was relative. The help we employed were making fifteen dollars a week.

"On Maxwell Street, everything was a specialty store. There was no such thing as a supermarket. It was either a bakery, a butcher shop, a fish market, or a chicken store where they had chicken coops on the sidewalk. You wanted chickens, you'd take the chicken out, they'd take it in the back, they'd kill it, and you had chicken. We were just one of the many stores in the area."

BEN AND CELE LYON ON MAXWELL STREET, C. 1940. Ben married the landlord's daughter in 1933. (Courtesy of Ben Lyon.)

Ben Lyon's father died in 1937, his mother in 1953. He ran the business. His sons would help out, but it was Ben and hired employees that made the business work.

One of those employees was Nate Duncan. Nate was about sixteen years old when he started working for Ben Lyon.

"I started working for Ben Lyon in 1947," recalled Duncan, an African-American who would eventually take over the business and remain in operation until the University of Illinois at Chicago bought him out and demolished the entire block.

"How I got the job is, I was not good in school. I couldn't do nothing in those years. My mother made me either go to school or work. And I had an aunt that worked for them in those years, and she got that job for me with them, and that's how I started with Ben Lyon."

For Nate Duncan, the job at Lyon's Delicatessen would be the only truly significant employment he ever needed. Not only was it a job, it was an education that included his learning to speak and understand Yiddish fluently. Many a customer did a double-take when they heard Nate say something like, "*Gebakte Leber*? You want chopped liver? OK."

"It was beautiful," said Nate. "I enjoyed working, and I guess everything about that store was enjoyable. You went to work at eight o'clock in the morning and you stayed, at least two days a week, until nine o'clock at night. And most of the Jewish guys used to come in there and sit around in the evening and talk. That's how I learned about a lot of things. I could tell you things that happened before I was born by listening to all the old Jewish guys. And that was very interesting."

The closeness between Ben Lyon and Nate Duncan grew and was extraordinary.

"I don't think there was a nicer fellow in the world than the guy I was working for," said Nate. "Never had an argument with him out of all those twenty-five years. And if I did something childish he'd explain it to me. If I went to buy something, he'd tell me how to do it, how to save money, or give me the money to do it and let me pay him back however I could. He was a wonderful fella."

"Nate was busy all day making coffee," Ben remembered. "He made eggs like nobody can, scrambled eggs. I don't know how he did it, but he learned and he had a certain knack about making scrambled eggs or regular omelets. It was just terrific".

Nate Duncan also learned to make Sara Lyon's pickled herring. (Look for the recipe at the end of this story.) "Nobody really taught me," said Nate. "I just used to watch her. As she would go and make it, I would just stand and watch her. Matter of fact, Ben Lyon didn't know how to make any of that stuff. I learned from his mother."

"My mother showed him how to make pickled herring, and he became quite expert at it," said Ben. "And, they didn't want my mother's herring anymore, they wanted Nate's herring. Everybody knew Nate and everybody liked him."

NATE DUNCAN, *2003* AND IN THE *1980S*.
*He started working for Ben Lyon in 1947 and,
except for military service, never worked anywhere
but the delicatessen. When Ben retired, he sold
the business to Nate. (Courtesy of Nate Duncan.
2003 Photo by Roger Schatz.)*

NATE'S DELICATESSEN IN THE EARLY 1990S. *Nate's Delicatessen is seen here not long before the building was bought by the University of Illinois at Chicago and demolished. Nate Duncan never changed the menu after Ben Lyon retired. It was always a kosher restaurant and continued to do a brisk business. Patrons would come from out-of-state to get some of Nate's pickled herring, which he learned to make from Ben Lyon's mother. (Photo by Steven Balkin, courtesy of Nate Duncan.)*

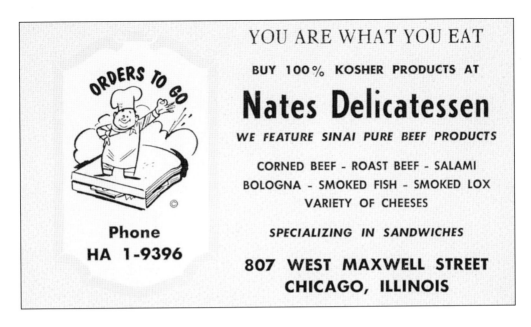

YOU ARE WHAT YOU EAT

BUY 100% KOSHER PRODUCTS AT

Nates Delicatessen

WE FEATURE SINAI PURE BEEF PRODUCTS

CORNED BEEF - ROAST BEEF - SALAMI
BOLOGNA - SMOKED FISH - SMOKED LOX
VARIETY OF CHEESES

SPECIALIZING IN SANDWICHES

807 WEST MAXWELL STREET
CHICAGO, ILLINOIS

ORDERS TO GO

Phone
HA 1-9396

NATE'S BUSINESS CARD. (Courtesy of Nate Duncan.)

In 1973, Cele Lyon died. She had a stroke three years earlier and it was then Ben started thinking of retirement. Nate Duncan was the obvious successor for the business.

"When it came down to retiring, I sat down with Nate. I said, 'Do you want to take over the store, Nate? You can take it. You don't have to give me any money. You can pay it off. And I'll establish a little credit for you.'"

Ben took Nate to meet his bankers. Nate got the business. When Nate paid off his debt, Ben sold him the building for twelve-thousand dollars. While it made perfect business sense to offer Nate the business, the way it was accomplished was, for Ben Lyon, a *mitzvah.*

"Nate was well-liked by everybody, and he knew everybody and everybody knew him," said Ben. "I knew he would do well. He would make money right from the beginning. Everything worked out good for him, and worked out good for me."

Lyon's Delicatessen became Nate's Deli.

"There was talk around that I would never make it," said Nate. "They said, 'He wouldn't be there a good year and he gotta start putting stuff in there that's not kosher and hamburgers and all that stuff,' which I never did. The whole time I had that store, the only thing I ever had there was all kosher food. I was certainly more familiar with that than I was other foods, so I kept it exactly like it was when he was there, and I maintained it all until I closed."

The pickled herring remained, as well.

"I used to have all the Jewish ladies coming in my store trying to get my recipe how to make that herring. I never would give it to 'em, I wouldn't give it to 'em. I never give my recipe to anyone. I did teach my mother how to make it. I sold a lot of herring. The late Chicago Mayor Michael Bilandic used to always get it. A lot of senators and stuff like that used to come by, and I used to have to make them a whole case, $12 a case."

Nate's Deli was in business until the City of Chicago moved into the area in early 1994, claiming eminent domain, as it did throughout the market. Nate sold his property and although the land was quickly cleared, it wasn't for another six years that the University of Illinois at Chicago began developing the site.

NATE'S DELI AND THE BLUES BROTHERS. *In 1980, Nate's Deli was the locale for one of the more memorable scenes in the feature film,* The Blues Brothers. *Singer Aretha Franklin performed a rollicking musical number called "Think", with actors Dan Aykroyd and John Belushi. Aykroyd posed with Nate and others during a break in the production. (Courtesy of Nate Duncan.)*

In the 1930s, when African Americans began moving up from the South into Chicago's South Side, the distinctly Jewish atmosphere on Maxwell Street became, as well, a locale for the Blues. Musicians, mostly black, some white, roamed the shopping areas performing and hoping a few dollars would be offered before the end of the day. By the 1950s and even until the last days, Maxwell Street was a Blues center. Many of the famous and not so famous Blues musicians played on Maxwell Street, and, as Nate remembered, stopped to play and then eat at the deli.

For posterity, besides the old photographs of Nate's, Hollywood did help keep the old place alive when the deli was used for one of the musical scenes in the 1980 film *The Blues Brothers.* Singer Aretha Franklin and actors John Belushi and Dan Aykroyd, performed a memorable, somewhat uninhibited number entitled, "Think."

Nate Duncan first saw Maxwell Street in the 1930s. He worked there all his life. He understood the attachment that the Blues had to the area. But, it is clear to Nate how Maxwell Street should be remembered.

"You can't stop progress, but they should have saved a portion of that street for the history . . . not the Blues, not for the Blues. It's for the Jewish history that they should have saved that street."

Sara Lyon's Secret Recipe for Pickled Herring

The recipe has never been made public. In fact, Nate Duncan says Mrs. Lyon never wrote it down and neither did he. But the pickled herring from Lyons/Nate's Delicatessen was a Maxwell Street favorite. People came from all over to stock up. Nate Duncan said that he still gets calls from former customers pleading with him to make a batch just for them. Nate, in fact, complied with some of those requests, but at 73 doesn't want to bother anymore. When asked to provide the recipe for this book, he agreed. Ben Lyon had no objection. In fact he said, "Why not?"

The secret is in the vinegar and sugar.

Ingredients

> Shmaltz Herring
> Vinegar
> Pickeling Spices
> Sugar
> Onion

Cut and clean herring, inside and out.
Place in cold water.
Change water three times to remove salt.
Place in refrigerator for two days.
On second day, cut each herring into five pieces.
Cut onion very thin and place on top of herring pieces.
Mix pure white Heinz vinegar with sugar. Vinegar should be more sweet than sour.
Pour mixture onto herring, making sure fish pieces are well-covered.
Place pickeling spices into a piece of cheese cloth and place atop herring.
Pour one cup of vinegar through cheese cloth let soak with spices.
Place in refrigerator for 4 to 5-days.

Leavitt's Deli and Restaurant

In 1920, if Sam Levin, owner of Sinai Kosher Sausage Company, hadn't agreed to loan the Leavitt brothers 18,000 dollars, and if a prominent Christian Science pharmacist named Doctor Frank Stahl hadn't agreed to rent his building exactly on the northwest corner of Maxwell Street and Halsted, Chicago might never have experienced the famous Leavitt's Delicatessen and Restaurant.

Maxwell Street's first generation Leavitt brothers, Sam, Louis, Isadore, Nathan, Maurice, Frank, and Harry, had operated a clothing business for a few years, but had to close-out. They didn't have enough capital after all the bills were paid, but wanted to start a new enterprise on Maxwell Street. With the loan, they'd open a grocery and restaurant. Sam

SAM LEAVITT, 1940s.

SOL LEAVITT. Sol and his brothers took over the business after Sam's death in 1945. (Courtesy of Shirley Leavitt.)

LEAVITT'S DELICATESSEN AND RESTAURANT, 1955. *Leavitt's Delicatessen and Restaurant was a fixture on the northwest corner of Maxwell and Halsted Streets from the 1920s until the business was sold in the 1960s. Sam Leavitt and his five brothers opened up after getting a loan from the owner of Sinai Kosher Sausage Company. Terms of the loan included using only Sinai products. (Courtesy of Chicago Historical Society.)*

Levin, the Sinai Kosher Sausage owner gave the loan, with the condition that the Leavitt's buy all of their meat products from him. So, what became the famous Leavitt's kosher hot dogs, salami, and corn beef were written into the loan contract.

It wasn't all that easy to become a Chicago institution and a centerpiece of Maxwell Street. It took a lot more than just delicious hot dogs with grilled onions and mustard, and an aroma that never went away.

There is a hand-written journal about the Leavitt family's history in America and in Chicago. It was lovingly written by Sol Leavitt, one of Sam Leavitt's six children. Sol's

SOL LEAVITT'S HANDWRITTEN JOURNAL. *This copy of Sol Leavitt's handwritten journal details the history of the family's long ownership of the deli and restaurant. The Leavitt's also owned various liquor businesses. (Journal courtesy of Shirley Leavitt. Photo by Roger Schatz.)*

widow, Shirley, provided excerpts from the journal for this book. There is more than just a warm story about a large family in Sol Leavitt's memoirs. There emerges also, a detailed account of entrepreneurship, doing business during the Depression, innovation, meeting obligations, and decades of very hard work.

Here is part of Sol Leavitt's Maxwell Street story.

A large space that previously had contained a clothing store was in the building at 1320 South Halsted Street. It was 1920 and Sol's father Sam, and Sam's brothers were about to try a new venture.

"The lease with Doctor Stahl was signed and somehow they had the clothing store remodeled and opened the store which became the famous Leavitt brothers. Since they had no capital, they took advantage of their lease to sublet two stores on the Maxwell Street side and at 1318 South Halsted. They even leased the new deli counter to a man, Hymie Karm, knowledgeable in that line, for the first year only. They operated the grocery and fruit and vegetable department. The rent income was sufficient to pay the entire rent and allowed them to make a living in the store, working six days a week and many hours each day."

"Lewis and Sam had made a deal with Sinai to return the loan by applying their volume discounts to the loan. When the loan was finally repaid, they continued to receive the discount in the form of a credit memo toward their monthly purchases. During the

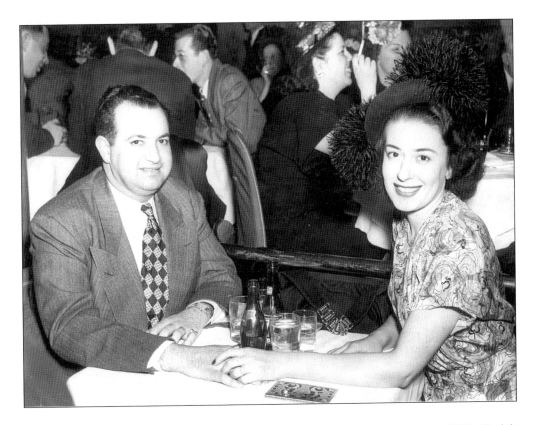

SOL MARRIED SHIRLEY LEAVITT IN 1947. *She had worked for the Leavitt's during World War II while Sol was in the Army. (Courtesy of Shirley Leavitt.)*

SHIRLEY LEAVITT, 2002. *(Photo by Roger Schatz.)*

SOL LEAVITT BEHIND THE BAR. *Sol was 18 years old when the bar was opened the moment Prohibition ended in 1933. He remembers each barrel of draught beer held 400, ten-ounce servings, and that scores of barrels were emptied that first night. (Courtesy of Shirley Leavitt.)*

Depression, in the 1930s, the price of delicatessen meats was very low. Mr. Levin and Charley Posen merged his Posen's Kosher Star Sausage into Sinai, along with Newberry Kosher, Palestine Kosher, and Best Kosher. The conglomerate of all the kosher factories in Chicago curtailed part of the discount. Salami and hot dogs were as low as 17 cents a pound and the ten percent monthly discount credit plus two cents per pound, brought the price down below 14 cents. Mr. Posen once remarked that, 'What if Salami went down to two cents per pound. You'd be getting it free.'

"The Depression years of the '30s caused the Leavitt brothers to go into debt, paying interest rates of six to eight percent, when the banks were paying two and a-half to three percent on savings. Their loans were from private people, and they did not return these loans until the boom, war years of the early 1940s."

Shirley Leavitt held back tears when she read the next line of her husband's journal.

"But, every creditor was paid-in-full."

Sol Leavitt spent World War II as an artillery spotter in Europe. It was during the war years that the family business was finally making the kind of income that brought the Leavitt's some solid economic security. Part of the reason for that, Sol said in his journal, was the high cost of meat, and the great value and demand on liquor.

Leavitt's Delicatessen and Restaurant had been selling liquor from the very moment Prohibition ended. The fruit and vegetable section was phased out when the restaurant, with a soda fountain, opened. A large cigar counter divided the deli and restaurant.

That was the business when booze became legal again.

"In 1933, Prohibition Law was repealed," Sol wrote. "The long counter that was a soda fountain and all the grocery section were remodeled into a long mahogany bar opposite the delicatessen counter."

The Leavitt brothers had applied for and received the proper city, state and federal licenses to operate a retail liquor, beer, and wine establishment. Their decision to go into the liquor business was a wise one. Based on the fact that the retail grocery and produce business barely made expenses and required hard work.

Sol was 18-years old when Prohibition ended.

"I, Sol, remember the first night that beer was sold. The bar sold many barrels that night. Four hundred glasses of draught, ten ounces each, per barrel, retailing at ten cents a glass. The deli counter was kept busy selling sandwiches for the drinkers. Ten cents for salami sandwiches and fifteen cents for corn beef sandwiches. The bartender would take the order for the sandwiches and send them across to the deli counter by the home-made wire trolley car. Sandwiches were put on plates and on to the car, made to hold three at a time, and pushed across with one push. These trolley baskets were made by our expert deli man Max Karm, who had been trained in Russia in sheet metal work. He was an expert mechanic in cutting and welding stainless steel. New customers were amazed by the contraptions. He had several going across going overhead."

Liquor was back and the Leavitt's opened another bar, liquor store, and restaurant directly south, across Maxwell Street.

"This operation was known as Roosevelt Liquors. Roosevelt Road was one block away. Franklin Roosevelt was president, and one of the brothers, Maurice, had private labels made with a rough sketch of Theodore Roosevelt's face, and such names as "Colonel Teddy" and "Rough Rider," showing Theodore Roosevelt on horseback. One day a letter comes from the family and heirs of Theodore Roosevelt ordering us to cease and desist using these obvious references to Theodore Roosevelt."

The Leavitt's ceased and desisted. However, the Leavitt brothers continued in the liquor business at various locations for many years.

During World War II, the boost in business and prices brought on by shortages and rationing, allowed the Leavitt's to buy the real estate they'd been renting for over 20 years.

"Finally, the Leavitt brothers were able to pay up all debts, buy the properties at 1320 and 1330 South Halsted, and for the first time in business had surpluses, cash, and interest income instead of usuries."

Sol's father, Sam died in 1945. He was 59 years old. Sol and his brothers would eventually take over the business and carry on. Sol married Shirley in 1947, and the deli and restaurant remained a Maxwell Street landmark. The business remained on Maxwell Street when a new owner, Jim Stefanovic, leased the property in 1973 and operated under the name, "Jim's Original" until the wrecking ball swung. "Jim's" has operated since, one block east on Union Avenue, and expects to return to Maxwell Street in one of the few old buildings the University of Illinois at Chicago preserves.

Ι t was not the kind of necktie usually found on Maxwell Street.

The rope was real, so was the noose.

Initiation into the new block club formed by ten-year-old Abe Drexler and his friends in 1920 in the Maxwell Street area, required that each new member be lifted by his neck two stories up. Abe went first. His friends yanked him from the street up to a second floor window.

It was a fluke that Abe wasn't killed or hurt. It was no fluke that no one else wanted to be initiated.

So it was that Abe Drexler, whose family ran a fruit and vegetable stand, got the name "Fluky." It stuck. Boy how it stuck!

In 1929, Jacob Drexler, Fluky's father, converted part of the fruit and vegetable business into a hot dog stand called Fluky's right in front of Leavitt's Restaurant and Delicatessen, on the northwest corner of Maxwell and Halsted. It was a small shack, really, about 15-feet wide with shingle-like openings on three sides, built partially in the street and on the sidewalk, atop a fire hydrant that provided the stand's water supply.

"My grandfather named the stand after my dad because Fluky Drexler was a popular guy," said Jack Drexler, Fluky's son.

In fact, Abe "Fluky" Drexler was a very personable young man, as well as an accomplished athlete. He had been an All-City basketball player at Medill High School and even pitched a one-hitter in a high school baseball game played at Wrigley Field.

He was also very funny.

"During the 1930s," Jack explained, "my father would go to the night clubs on Madison Street and they'd take him out of the audience to M.C. shows. It wasn't until I was in my 30s that I heard my father tell the same joke twice."

Jack Drexler would follow his father into the hot dog business, and in fact was the force behind ensuring the name Fluky's would remain a Chicago institution, when he opened a Fluky's on the north side at Pratt and Western Avenue in 1964. That site remains the flagship business. Having worked with his dad at Fluky's stands at Van Buren and Canal and Harrison and Canal in the early 60s, Jack heard the stories of Maxwell Street.

"My dad would make his own orangeade on Maxwell Street. Making the orangeade, he would use the water from the fire hydrant, and that came right from the city and that had sand in it. So, when people complained that the orangeade was gritty, he told them he used real oranges and that's pulp. So people said, 'This is great!'

"One time some Italian kids from the Taylor Street area held up a bank in Milwaukee and they hid the money and the guns under my dad's hot dog stand. There was no locking up your stand at night, so they just lifted the window and hid the guns and money. It's not like you have a building where you have to have a door to get in. My dad didn't know it until they got caught and went to jail and the police came and got the guns and the money."

Then, there is the case of the mustard jar and the pistol.

"Somebody ran by and threw a gun up on the counter. My dad took the gun and opened up a mustard jar and threw the gun in the mustard jar, shook it up and left it there. He didn't know; he didn't have a clue, didn't have an idea where it came from or what happened. All he knew was one day the mustard jar disappeared."

The Vienna Beef Company had a manufacturing plant on the east side of Halsted Street, between Roosevelt and Maxwell. Deliveries of hot dogs to Fluky's was often done, literally, on the shoulder's of the company's executive vice president, a man Jack Drexler identified as Henry Davis.

On Maxwell Street a Fluky's Hot Dog originally cost a nickel. That included the pickles, lettuce, onions, tomatoes, cucumbers, celery salt, and the usual condiments. Anyone from Chicago identifies such a feast as a true Chicago hot dog. It was a huge success at the World's Fair in 1933. Fluky's doesn't take credit for inventing such a banquet in a bun, but Abe Drexler had good reason to pile on the goodies.

"Because my grandfather had this little vegetable and fruit stand, when they started making hot dogs, they started putting the vegetables and everything else on there," said Jack. "That's how we created it."

Grilled onions, Jack noted, came later, when gas-fired stoves were added. Initially, hot dogs

OPENING OF FLUKY'S. *Abe and Esther Drexler and their son Jack are pictured here at the opening of the Fluky's restaurant on Western and Pratt Avenue on Chicago's North Side in 1964. As many as five Fluky's restaurants operated at the same time. Abe sold the Maxwell Street stand to his brother in 1944. (Courtesy of Jack Drexler.)*

ABE "FLUKY" DREXLER AND HIS WIFE ESTHER, 1942. *Abe's father, Jacob, opened Fluky's hot dog stand in 1929. He used his son's nickname because his son was a very popular figure on Maxwell Street. "Fluky" ran the business, located directly in front of Leavitt's Restaurant. (Courtesy of Jack Drexler.)*

were cooked in water. Fluky's on Maxwell Street was always busy. Jack says his father told him as many as eight or nine people worked the stand selling from the three open sides, when the crowds were large.

As many as five Fluky's operated at any one time. And, in all the locations, the customers kept coming in large numbers. Even the famous customers.

"Over the years, we've had so many celebrities come to Fluky's," said Jack.

"The comedian Steve Allen, when he used to go for his piano lesson when he was a kid, used to transfer at Roosevelt and Halsted, and he used to stop at Fluky's. Shekky Green, Shelley Berman, Joey Bishop, it goes on and on. Even in my era, I've had a good number of the Second City people."

Jack said that Bernie Salins, the founder of Second City, has walked from Wells and North Avenue to *Fluky's* on Western and Pratt. That's about ten miles.

"Even Jimmy Carter came in," Jack said proudly. "A fellow named Moscowitz, who was one of his people here in Chicago, brought him in for lunch."

Wolfy's, another well-known hot dog vendor in Chicago, originally was started by one of Jack Drexler's cousins who could have used the name Fluky's. Jack said his cousin thought that somehow hot dogs and Wolfy's seemed to go together.

Abe Drexler operated Fluky's on Maxwell Street until 1944, when he sold it to his brother, Ben, who also was known as "Irish" because of his association with two Irish mobsters named Drugan and Lake. Among some of the other Fluky's locations over the years, were stores at Roosevelt Road and Central Avenue, Lincoln and Ogden, 63rd and Blackstone and Sheridan Road at Pratt.

Fluky Drexler died on Thanksgiving Day in 1986. He taught his son well, not only the Maxwell Street stories, but about the business. Today, Jack Drexler still operates the *Fluky's* at Pratt and Western, and two others, in the Lincolnwood Town Center and the Nordstrom's Atrium on Michigan Avenue. Since 1989, hot dogs at Fluky's are made by the Drexler company in Milwaukee, and there is a full-line of Fluky's all beef products sold in more than one hundred grocery stores. The company is also a supplier of private label meat products.

Maybe it was no fluke after all.

GOLD'S RESTAURANT

There were many places to eat on Maxwell Street. Everyone seems to remember the aroma of hot dogs. And while Lyon's Delicatessen and Levitt's Restaurant were Maxwell Street icons catering to other tastes besides hot dogs, there was one place nearby, on Roosevelt Road and just west of Halsted that was extra special.

"My father owned Gold's Restaurant," said Shirlee Mages. She married her husband, Morrie Mages at Gold's.

"It was beautiful," Shirlee remembered. "Every one of the weddings there was beautiful. It was gorgeous. The food was absolutely marvelous. That's why everybody got married there.

"In those days," Shirlee went on, "almost every Jewish person was married at Gold's Restaurant upstairs at the banquet hall."

Gold's was one of the first restaurants anywhere near Maxwell Street or even the Loop, with air conditioning and valet parking service.

"Any Jewish celebrity that was in Chicago was at my father's restaurant every single night. I met Sophie Tucker there, I met George Jessel there, I met Al Jolson, I met the Great Houdini there. They were there constantly."

Gold's was a 24-hour operation, so the show business types were not the only patrons.

GOLD'S RESTAURANT. *Shirlee Gold's father, Meyer, owned Gold's Restaurant, the "in" place for weddings, bar mitzvahs, and other occasions. Jewish celebrities the likes of Al Jolson and George Jessel would stop in whenever they were in Chicago. It was a nighttime hangout for Al Capone and other mobsters. Gold's was on the north side of Roosevelt Road, just west of Halsted Street. The University of Illinois at Chicago's baseball fields are on the site today. (Courtesy Chicago Transit Authority.)*

MAXWELL STREET MARRIAGES. *Marriages among children of Maxwell Street merchants were very common. Shirlee Gold married Morrie Mages at her father's restaurant. (Courtesy of the Mages Family.)*

"At night, all the gangsters used to come in. Al Capone and his mob were there almost every single night."

Shirlee Mages is especially proud that the "King of Swing" got his start at Gold's Restaurant. "Benny Goodman started his orchestra at my father's restaurant. He said, 'Mr. Gold, can I use your banquet hall upstairs to practice? There's three of us, and we have no place to practice.' And my father said, 'Of course, any time.' So, he came about three, four times a week, three of them practicing. Then after a few months, there were five of them and they were practicing constantly. After a few more months, there were seven of them and Benny Goodman came to my father, and he said, 'Mr. Gold, we just got a date in New York for my band. I don't think I'll need your hall upstairs anymore.' And that was the beginning of the Benny Goodman Orchestra."*

*From several sources on Jazz and Big Band music, it can be surmised that Benny Goodman's first New York appearance with the orchestra that practiced at Gold's was probably in 1934, at Billy Rose's Music Hall, and shortly thereafter on the "Let's Dance," radio series. Goodman had played in New York as a free-lance musician as early as 1929, but earliest references to his orchestra fit the 1934 timeline. Goodman was born in 1909. His childhood home was at 1342 West Washburne, less than a mile from Maxwell and Halsted Streets.

BENNY GOODMAN. *The "King of Swing," Benny Goodman, started his first band at Gold's Restaurant. At the time, Goodman lived close to Gold's and Maxwell Street, on the 1300 block of west Washburn Avenue. (Courtesy of The Chicago Historical Society. 1938 photo from archives of the* Chicago Herald Examiner.*)*

GOLD'S DITTO

Both of Alan Lapping's grandfathers were well-known in their time on Maxwell Street. One was the blind market master, Harry Lapping, noted in a previous section of this book. But, his other grandfather worked for Shirlee Gold Mages' father. He underscored what Mrs. Mages said about Gold's Restaurant.

"My other grandfather was the night manager at Gold's Restaurant and was there until the close probably in the middle '60s or early '70s. My mother and dad were married there, my sister-in-law was married there, and it was the social capital of the city in those days."

MEYER DAVIS

Another popoular Maxwell Street restaurant in the '30s and '40s was a delicatessen at Maxwell and Newberry called Meyer Davis.

"Meyer Davis was my grandfather," said Allan Davis. "My father worked in the restaurant cutting cabbage all day to make coleslaw. When my father thought he was finished, my grandfather would come and push the cut cabbage down into the crock and my father would have to start cutting all over again."

The coleslaw and the rest of the menu must have been good. After many years on Maxwell Street, Meyer Davis opened what became a very successful restaurant with the same name, further west at Roosevelt Road and Kedzie.

Allan Davis could eat free in some pretty good restaurants.

"My granduncle also had a restaurant. In the 1930's he opened Ashkenosh in Rogers Park. It was one of the very popular restaurants there for decades."

MODERN PERFECTION

Lillian Stein and her sister Paulette Kallow insist their father had a monopoly on the sale of soda pop and seltzer water on Maxwell Street.

Sol Goldstein established the Modern Perfection Bottling Company during the Prohibition Era (1919–1933) and his daughters claim he had the political connections—the clout—to keep any other bottler out of the market area.

"Our father had the entire Maxwell Street area for pop," Paulette said proudly. "No one else could go in and sell soda water there, only my father."

The family had earned a living with a tavern and grocery business at 1347 South Jefferson Street. Then, in 1919, came the Volsted Act and Prohibition on alcoholic beverages. Selling soft drinks was an obvious alternative to bathtub gin.

The bottling plant was on O'Brien Street, right in the heart of the neighborhood. Lillian and Paulette said Modern Perfection Bottling offered orange, strawberry, root beer, and other flavors, but not all were available at Passover.

Before Peysach (Passover) the bottles have to be koshered, and there was no nonsense about it. They had to bring in new bottles and could only use certain flavors, because, God forbid, you couldn't use certain flavors at Peysach time," said Lillian.

"The sugar had to be fresh. So my father goes and makes the whole factory, the entire factory peysachdik (kosher for Passover). I mean he had to close down, he had to scrub, they had to clean, then he brings the pop in the house and my mother says, 'I'm not sure it was really peysachdik.' I thought he'd kill her," added Paulette.

"We were the most popular house on Independence Boulevard," laughed Paulette. "We had the pop and nobody could afford, in those days, to have soda in their home. So, we were so popular, we didn't know what water tasted like."

7.

Roller Derby King and Other Stories
HELL ON WHEELS

Adm. Hyman Rickover, Supreme Court Justice Arthur Goldberg, Actor Paul Muni, and CBS owner William Paley may all be Maxwell Street kids, but none could skate like Sammy Skobel.

Barney Ross could take a punch and King Levinsky could take one occasionally. But, neither of those Maxwell Street natives could do the Whip like "Slammin'" Sammy Skobel, rolling around the 45 degree banked track at Madison Square Garden in New York City. None could be a jammer like Sammy, on the rink at the old Chicago Coliseum on South Wabash Avenue. Sammy Skobel was so good on skates that he wound up in the Roller Derby Hall of Fame, a long way from where he was born, in 1926, at 1017 West Maxwell Street.

Sammy was not Jewish. However, like so many of the Jewish immigrants, his family had come from Russia to find a better life. His story, his life, is an obvious example that anyone who grabbed hold of the opportunities that the Maxwell Street environment offered, could partake significantly in the promise of America. Certainly whoever you were, it helped to have a strong, loving family to make the best of the opportunities. Sammy Skobel had that love and support.

"My parents owned Skobel Grocery, Meat Market and Catering in the same building where I was born," Sammy said. "They were there until 1956.

"When I didn't work in the store, I roller-skated around the Maxwell Street area with my shoeshine box. Starting in 1934, when I was eight years old, I shined the shoes of the police officers at the Maxwell Street police station before they had to line up for morning inspection. I charged them two cents a shine."

Sammy joined the Roller Derby in 1945, after graduating from Crane Tech High School. For the next 20 years, he was one of the true stars of the game, playing six years for the Brooklyn Red Devils, a team he also coached. He played two years with the New York Chiefs, and was on their world championship team. He finished his career in Chicago, skating for 12 years with the Chicago Westerners.

Some might say Sammy Skobel was so good he could do it with his eyes closed.
In fact, he almost did.

"I'm legally blind," Sammy laughed. "I lost my sight at the age of four due to scarlet fever which affected the optic nerves in both of my eyes. I lost over 90 percent of my sight."

Sammy explained how he managed to fly around the roller rink for so long, and to become one of the greats of his sport.

"There were six teams in the league. We had an 86 game season, playing about five games a week. The season started in October and ran until June. Everything I saw was just a blur, but I memorized the body frames. I could tell who was who because I knew what their body looked like. I knew their style."

SAMMY SKOBEL, ON LEFT, AS CAPTAIN OF THE BROOKLYN RED DEVILS. *Skobel was inducted into the Roller Derby Hall of Fame after a career with Brooklyn, the New York Chiefs, and the Chicago Westerners. Almost blind from a childhood bout with scarlet fever, he learned to skate on Maxwell Street, moving block to block shining shoes. (Courtesy of Sammy Skobel.)*

Given that each team had about 30 identically uniformed skaters, men and women, Sammy had to memorize a lot of bodies. He also managed to set the world's one-mile skating record. He did that at Madison Square Garden, covering the 5,280 feet in two minutes 33 seconds. The record, set in 1958, still stands.

"Wherever I skated in the world, when I told them I was from Chicago, they said, 'Do you know anything about Maxwell Street?' And I told them my story, how I was born on the street, where you could get a screw driver to a mink coat. It was a perfect place for people to shop during the Depression."

Sammy published an autobiography in 1984, *Semka, The Sammy Skobel Story*. The influence of Maxwell Street is everywhere in the book.

He founded the Illinois chapter of the American Blind Skiing Foundation, and has become an avid golfer. A guy like Sammy is obviously in demand to speak to young people.

"I tell them you can achieve any goal that you want to in life if you believe you can, if you have the desire and determination. I tell them, if you have the discipline, you can achieve anything that you want to in life. And that was Maxwell Street to me. I learned it first on Maxwell Street."

THE CHOCOLATE FLOOD

Seymour DeKoven hated to come down and work at this father's Maxwell Street drugstore. He would help out, doing all kinds of tasks in the store, but from the time he started doing so, in 1930, he really wanted to do something else.

"Ever since I was ten years old, my older sister and I . . . she is three years older than I am . . . used to go every Saturday and Sunday to the drugstore with my father and work. And I always hated it because I couldn't play with my friends." But, Seymour and Anita DeKoven honored their father, Jacob's wishes, and went to work.

Jacob DeKoven was born in a small Russian village and came to Chicago in 1905 when he was 17 years old. His brother, a doctor, gave him the money to attend pharmacy school. In 1907, Jacob DeKoven, again with his brother's help, signed a lease and opened DeKoven Drugs at 1301 South Halsted, right on the northeast corner of Halsted and Maxwell.

"The drugstore had perhaps one or two pharmacists working for my father. It was quite small, but my father ran it successfully for many, many years," Seymour said.

In the old days on Maxwell Street, or just about anywhere else, drugstores that had soda fountains usually had to make their own ingredients for the tasty treats on the menu. At the DeKoven store, Seymour made the chocolate syrup, and was responsible for possibly, the most delicious flood Maxwell Street ever saw.

SEYMOUR DEKOVEN AND HIS SISTER ANITA, 1926. *They wanted to play with their friends but worked in their father's Maxwell Street drug store instead. (Courtesy of Seymour DeKoven.)*

JACOB DEKOVEN. *Seymour's father, Jacob DeKoven, opened DeKoven's Drug Store in 1907 at 1301 South Halsted. Seymour made chocolate syrup in the basement for the soda fountain in the store. The store was closed in 1947, but Seymour and other relatives created a chain of stores elsewhere in the Chicago area and operated departments within drug stores in several states. (Courtesy of Seymour DeKoven.)*

"In the basement of the drugstore, in order to make chocolate, you had a huge pot on a stove, a gas stove. You had to keep stirring it and stirring it in order to make chocolate syrup for the sodas we sold at the six-seat fountain in the front of the store. And I remember once, my father called me. He needed me upstairs. So, I came running up the stairs, and totally forgot about the fact that I was stirring the chocolate syrup. The thing went all over the place. It flooded the basement with chocolate syrup."

After 40 years, the drug store closed in 1947. But, it was from that Maxwell Street business that Seymour DeKoven and other family members would eventually expand into a chain of drugstores, as well as, operate various departments within drugstores in ten states.

MAXWELL AND HALSTED STREETS, 1920S. *DeKoven's is located on the northeast corner of the intersection of this east looking view. (Courtesy of Seymour DeKoven.)*

Not only could you cut a deal on Maxwell Street you could cut a record. Bernard Abrams and his wife Idell sold and serviced radios, televisions, and other appliances in one of the two buildings that constituted Maxwell Radio and TV. In the other building, at 831 West Maxwell, the Abrams' operated a recording studio. The Abrams' also sold records and Bernard built his own brand of record players. That led to, certainly, a serendipitous start in the recording business. Idell remembers.

"He used to make phonographs out of the old floor model radios. He would make the phonograph in the bottom and a radio on top . . . In the early 1950s, someone came in to play a record on one of the phonographs. He left the record. Bern put it on the phonograph and after that he started doing recordings. He had this little Wilcox recorder and we recorded spiritual and blues. We would call them test records."

Most of the recording customers were African-American, mostly blues performers. But, others later made names for themselves as rock and rollers or in gospel music. Brook Benton, Little Walter, Muddy Waters, Johnny Williams, Howlin' Wolf, Mahalia Jackson, and the Staple Singers were some of the artists who cut test records, also called "demos" at Maxwell Radio and TV. Performers used the "demos" to approach the larger record companies, hoping some executive or producer would sign them to a contract.

In later years, some of those musicians and singers who cut their test records at Maxwell Radio and TV would return to thank Bernard Abrams for helping them out. Idell says her husband often couldn't remember what he had done to deserve the thanks.

"A guy came in with Little Walter, and he says, 'Bern, I want to thank you so much.' And my husband says, 'Well, for what?' And the guy says, 'Well, because you gave me a start when I needed a little hand-out. And I thank you very much for that.' There are just so many of those artists who came in, I couldn't even begin to tell you their names."

MAXWELL RADIO AND TV. Bernard Abrams sold radios, television, and other appliances at Maxwell Radio and TV, 831 West Maxwell. He started making recordings of blues musicians after a customer accidentally left a record in the store. (Courtesy of Idell Abrams.)

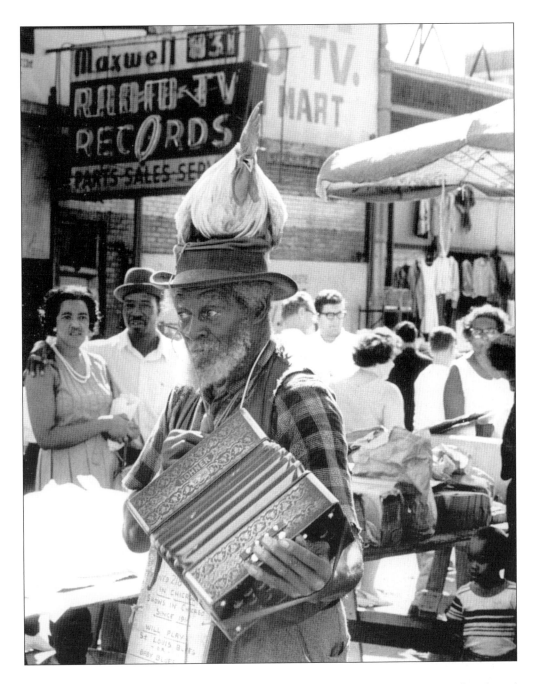

THE "CHICKEN MAN." *Maxwell Street's famed "Chicken Man" performing outside Maxwell Radio and TV in 1965. He said his name was Casey Jones and was born in 1870. He would have been 95-years old in this Jack Davis photograph. Many who had seen him on Maxwell Street reported he continued to perform with a chicken on the North Side of Chicago when he was past 100. (Courtesy of photographer Jack Davis.)*

Dialing for Booze

Abe Gorod had a drugstore on Maxwell Street in the first years after World War I, which were also the first years of Prohibition. Gorod was an uncle of Mildred Lerner, wife of the shoe dealer, Larry Lerner.

"Inside the drug store," laughed Larry, "they had a telephone booth for people who'd want to make a phone call. But, if you wanted to buy some booze during the Prohibition, you would go over to him and tell what you'd want. Then, he'd tell you to go into the telephone booth and make like you're making a telephone call. They had a sliding door in the telephone booth where he used to hand them the booze, and you'd put it in your pocket and go. That's how her uncle made a fortune."

"He made a lot of money," Mildred added. "He went back to Russia around 1920 or 1921. He made all this money during Prohibition, and he was able to go back to Russia where my parents lived, and my grandparents, and my sister. He brought his family to the United States."

The drugstore wasn't the only Maxwell Street locale where alcohol was available. Larry Lerner remembers how he learned there were more than just silent movies at the Globe Theatre on Maxwell Street.

"I found out that in the basement of the Globe, they had tracks, like street car tracks. And they used to bootleg liquor from the theatre to the Loop. All underground."

Turkey Skins

Mrs. Marian Shaw remembers that her physician father, Doctor Sherman L. Shapiro, made one 1940s Thanksgiving truly extraordinary.

"During the Second World War, the turkeys were going to the soldiers up front, so there were very few turkeys available. Dad went over to Maxwell Street and he came back holding two turkey skins. Mother filled up one skin with buckwheat dressing and the other with chestnuts. I remember dad in his pajamas sitting and cracking those chestnuts in the stove. We added chicken fat and the turkey skins would swell up so big and fine like bowling balls. Then, we sliced them and poured on gravy and that was our Thanksgiving."

Abe Kogan's Suit

There were many firsts on Maxwell Street: someone's first bicycle, their first nice dress, their first fur coat, their first really new pair of shoes.

For many men, going to Maxwell Street to buy their first suit was almost a right of passage. It was like that for Abe Kogan in the 1930s.

"When I was 12 years old and graduated from grade school, I was taken by my father and his two brothers to shop for my first suit. And they went to Maxwell Street. We went to a number of stores, we walked in and we walked out. Finally we went to one particular store on Halsted Street, about three doors south of Roosevelt Road. They haggled on the price and couldn't come to a conclusion. We walked out. A man right outside the store talked us back in, saying maybe we could get a better deal. We walked back into the store, the same thing happened again and we walked out again. The guy outside talked us back in again, but still we couldn't agree on a price. We walked out again. As we headed to another store, the guy outside started talking with the salesman and said loud enough for us to hear, 'you know what, maybe they've got the right price.' So, we went in a forth time and the deal was made and I had that suit.

"That was a gray sharkskin suit with two pair of pants and a vest, and I had that suit for a long, long time. I finished high school, I graduated college, I put in three years in the military, and I came home. I was engaged and thought I'd get married in that suit. But, my bride-to-be said to me, 'Abe, that suit is not for you.' And, ironically, I had finally grown into that suit. It fit me perfectly. But, I gave up the suit. I don't know what happened to it."

PANTS THIEF

Willie Goldstein has vivid memories of the pants thief.
"One time, when I was working on Maxwell Street, when I was a teen-ager, this guy runs out of Gabels (one of the larger clothing stores) with a pair of pants in his hands, and the salesman from Gabels runs out in his shorts and says, 'Hey, catch that guy, he's got my pants.' A puller from Sherwin's Clothing tackled the guy."

CHRIST, WHAT A PICTURE!

LoriLei Kramer's father, Isadore Gethner, sold his wares off a table on Maxwell Street.
"My dad sold plastic tablecloths. And then, later on, being an entrepreneur, he found out that pictures of Jesus Christ sold better than plastic tablecloths. So, he would recruit children of the neighborhood to help him put together these pictures with a glass frame bound together with tape."

SNAKE OIL

David Kolodny was born at 13th and Peoria. Maxwell Street was his world for a long time. So, if he says he remembers a snake oil salesman, why doubt him?
"He had a snake crawling all around his neck and his body," Mr. Kolodny said.
"He was selling special medicine. All of a sudden the snake took a bite out of his cheek. He closed up immediately and took off."

Kathy Kraas remembers her father, Sylvin Kraas, sold fruits and vegetables on Maxwell Street on Saturdays and Sundays. Mr. Kraas started selling on the streets in the 1930s, and continued until after World War II. He sang his pitch.

"I can say that all of my cousins, all of my family, and I can sing verbatim the aria that my father would sing on Maxwell Street every Saturday and Sunday."

Sylvin Kraas died in 2001. Saying her good-bye's at her father's funeral, Kathy sang her father's song.

> *Watermelons. Sweet and ripe. Watermelons.*
> *Sweet Bantam corn. Yellow.*
> *Buy 'em five cents a dozen."*

SYLVIN KRAAS (KRASNOWSKY). *Sylvin Kraas started selling goods on Maxwell Street while still in knickers. He would continue selling fruits and vegetables there until after World War II. (Courtesy of Midge Kraas.)*

KATHY KRAAS WITH HER FATHER, SYLVIN IN 1991. *In a tribute at his funeral, Kathy sang the song he would sing to pitch his wares on Maxwell Street. (Courtesy of Midge Kraas.)*

8.

Before the Colors Fade
WILLIAM W. GARFIELD

William W. Garfield's father took him to Maxwell Street regularly. His father, born Abraham W. Garfunkle, changed his name to Albert Garfield.

William's mother was Lutheran and wanted her son to go to church on Sundays. But, in 1957, when he turned eight years old, William began spending his Sundays on Maxwell Street.

"I guess I caught on and figured this to be more fun than church," Mr. Garfield wrote in a short memoir. "I loved cajoling dad into buying me things. I collected stamps so I usually found a vendor that sold stamps and dad would give me a couple bucks to spend. There were always toys—cheap toys that probably broke after a few uses, but it did not matter to me. Dad was buying me stuff. I was happy.

"I also obtained much of my fashionable wardrobe at Maxwell Street. A tube of about ten socks wrapped in box sealing tape, guaranteed to contain at least one pair with holes in them, cost about a buck.

"Shoes were best bought in one of the shops still standing in the late 1950s or early '60s. I remember the shoes tended to be stacked from floor to ceiling in no particular order, but as soon as you yelled out your size, the Jewish salesman would go right to them.

"There were few individual vendors that stand out in my memory. But, most memorable was Steve the Painter. Steve was a friendly black man who sold paint. My dad became very close with Steve and often hired him to paint our apartment. Steve the Painter also symbolizes in my mind, the transition period when the vendors changed from primarily Jewish to more black and Hispanic. I was no student of socio-economics then but, looking back, (I have an M.A. in City Planning) I now realize I was experiencing a major shift in this very important "port of entry" business incubator called Maxwell Street. Early Jewish immigrants saw Maxwell Street as a way to get a start in America. With little or no overhead… these folks could scrape out a meager living on the street. By the 1950s, most of the Jewish merchants had graduated, first, to the stores behind the street vendors and, second, to other businesses off of Maxwell Street—be it Wolfy's Hot Dogs or the President of CBS. It was now an opportunity for other disenfranchised minority groups to use Maxwell Street."

William Garfield's sojourns to the Maxwell Street area continued, even after the attraction for most had vanished. By the late 1980s, the area had become, for many, a slum. But, even as the University of Illinois at Chicago was putting up signage and light pole banners to promote its grand development plans, even as the demolition began, Garfield found Maxwell Street still pulling him in.

"Maxwell Street was a piece of real life. It was a piece of what America is really all about. It was working class people from disenfranchised ethnic groups, trying to carve out their little piece of the American dream. It was a beautiful cross-section of Americans that came

123

to shop there. You would see homeless people, common thieves, working class people of all ethnic backgrounds, middle class people, tourists, wealthy people, elderly children, families, Jews, Christians, you name it. I occasionally brought my daughter, Julia (born in 1987) there, what was left of it, from 1991 to '97. A couple people would ask me, 'Why would you bring your little daughter to that dangerous place?' My reply would be: 'Life is dangerous, life is reality, life is not some pretty single family home in the suburbs with a nice lawn and a plastic flamingo in the front yard. Maxwell Street represented real life—the good, the bad, the fun, the hardships, the best of people, the worst of people. Maxwell Street was my church, my institute of higher learning. Why wouldn't I bring my daughter there?' "

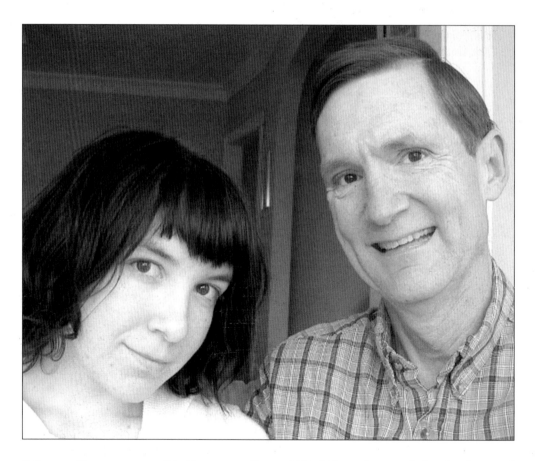

WILLIAM GARFIELD WITH HIS DAUGHTER JULIA, 2004. When Julia was a little girl and Maxwell Street had become known as an unsavory area, Garfield brought her on a visit. When asked why he'd take her to Maxwell Street, Garfield answered that the Street was his "church," his "institute of higher learning." He wanted her to understand. (Courtesy of William W. Garfield.)

9

Ode to Maxwell Street

SALLY LEVIN

The following poem was written by the late Sally Levin. It was first published by the *Chicago Jewish Sentinel* in February, 1987.

Mrs. Levin was born and raised in the Maxwell Street area. Her parents were Isaac and Bertha Yellin. Her father was a potato peddler and later ran Yellin's Grocery at Paulina Street and Roosevelt Road.

The poem was provided to the authors by Mrs. Levin's children, Mr. Marshall Levin and Mrs. Helen Goodfriend. Mrs. Levin died in 1992.

SALLY LEVIN. *(Courtesy of Helen Goodfriend.)*

Ode To Maxwell Street
As I Knew It

By Sally Levin

Maxwell Street is vanishing,
One of the last frontiers
Of the pioneers of pushcarts,
The heroes of immigrant years.

Here they came, the greenhorns,
Humble and God-fearing Jews
In search of a little Parnosoh, (livelihood)
The disinherited with nothing to lose

Lithuanian, Romanian, Polish, Galitzianer,
Pushing, shoving, peddling every ware.
This was the Golden America.
A joyous Laissez Faire.

You got to be an alrightnik,
With, "Mind you own business", "I don't care."
Not like by "Fonyeh Gonef" (a rascal, a thief)
With restrictions everywhere.

Peddlers shouted, "Vibaleh a Cholent," (Housewives, a stew)
"A-Tzimmis," (carrots) "A Carpaleh (carp) for Gefilte Fish,"
What a sweet aroma for Shabbos (Sabbath)
And the taste was so delish.

Halsted was for the big "Machers." (big shots)
Here the fancy stores would grow.
Here was the birth of an empire,
The start of the Nickel Show.

Admissions were two-for-a nickel.
How kids shivered with fear and delight
At William S. Hart in Cowboys and Indians
And the mysteries of lovely Pearl White.

The milliners were Mademoiselles from Slobodka
On whose best hats ostrich feathers would perch.
You were sure to look like Lillian Russell
As you strolled to synagogue or church.

Glickman's Yiddish Theatre
Was on Halsted and Fourteenth Street,
Where lonely souls of the Ghetto
Found a glorious musical treat.

The women thrilled to Boris Thomashefsky
And remembered him forevermore,
Recalling with vicarious pleasure
As they scrubbed the kitchen floor.

At the Maxwell Street Dispensary
You were treated fair and square
For ten cents you bought a ticket
And got excellent medical care.

Babies were born in abundance,
Obstetrics by Doctor DeLee.
Praise be to the Almighty
For this blessed care that was free.

On every block a synagogue,
Replicas of old shuls they had known,
Built with the pennies of peddlers
Who did not live by bread alone.

Gone with the wind is an era
Of few restrictions and frustrations
With twenty-five dollars you were in business
Without chain store strangulations.

Where are the inheritors
Of these brave, courageous men
Strong in their faith and spirit,
Shall we see their like again?

Gone are the sights and sounds of "Old Jew Town."
The new entrepreneurs are black and brown,
Free still to choose to work and scheme,
New pioneers of the American dream.

WRECKING BALL, MAXWELL STREET, 2001.

HISTORY.
PROGRESS.
MEMORIES.